THE SEARCH FOR FREEJOE

BY

EARNEST EDWARD LACEY

THIS BOOK IS DEDICATED TO:

GOD

AND

MY ANCESTORS

I HOPE I'VE DONE YOU PROUD

History with its flickering lamp stumbles along the trail of the past, trying to reconstruct its scenes, to revive its echoes, and kindle with pale gleams the passion of former days.

—*Sir Winston Churchill*

ISBN 0-9669076-0-4
Copyright 1999 by Earnest Edward Lacey
All rights reserved
Printed in the United States of America

FreeJoe Publications
Division of
FreeJoe Enterprises
P.O. Box 280786
Memphis, TN 38168
(901) 373-4770
Fax: (901) 373-4770

Cover and book design by Orin Carpenter

INTRODUCTION

"The Search For FreeJoe: tells the story of how I began to research the life of Joseph H. "FreeJoe" Harris, my great, great, great grandfather.

This journey back through time that began in Chicago, Illinois in August of 1984, has taken me to Goochland County, Virginia, Kalamazoo, Michigan and changed my permanant address from Chicago to Memphis, Tennessee.

The documents you see in this book came from the Courthouses and archives of Goochland County, Virginia and Memphis, Tennessee. They were used as a frame of reference in order to write my biographical novel, "FreeJoe: A Story of Faith, Love and Perseverance."

Many of the pictures in this book are of family members and people who played a role in the life of Joseph H. "FreeJoe" Harris and make up the characters in "FreeJoe: A Story of Faith, Love and Perseverance."

This book will show you the unusual accomplishments of Joseph H. "FreeJoe" Harris during the period of slavery and beyond. Perhaps these revelations will assist you in doing your family research.

This is the book that Alex Haley never wrote.

IN MEMORY OF:

JOE BRANCH

LILLIAN BEATRICE BRISCOE

IOLA LEWIS-BROOKS

DOLLY ABGAIL MCDONALD BROWN-DAVIS

JOE H. DAVIS

MARCELL PARHAM-GATEWOOD

ROBERT E. JOHNSON II

BERNICE EARNESTINE LEWIS-LACEY

VIRGE ALEXANDER LEWIS

MATTIE "PIE" FRANCES BOYD-MATTHEWS

LUCILLE ELAINE "NAN" JONES-ROBINSON

CLARENCE STOKES, JR.

ETHYL BELLE HORTON-VENSON

FLOSSIE BRANCH-WILSON

I HOPE I'VE DONE YOU PROUD

THE AUTHOR

Earnest Edward Lacey is the great, great, great grandson of Joseph "FreeJoe" Harris. Lacey began to research his family history 14 years ago while a resident of Chicago.

Lacey was born and raised in Memphis, Tennessee where he attended Melrose High School. He graduated from John Marshall High School, Loop Junior College (now Harold Washington Junior College) and Chicago State University in Chicago. He earned an MBA from Governors State University in University Park, Illinois.

He taught business and general educational courses at Prairie State Community College in Chicago Heights, Illinois, Olive-Harvey

Earnest Edward Lacey

Community College and Robert Morris College in Chicago, Illinois and LeMoyne College in Memphis, Tennessee. He is Director of the Tennessee Small Business Development Center at the University of Memphis. He serves as a business consultant counseling existing and start-up businesses. He is host of two television talk shows, Small Business Review and Ancestors.

Mr. Lacey is the author of the biographical novel *FreeJoe: A Story of Faith, Love and Perserverance*. He is a member of Gray's Creek Missionary Baptist Church in Eads, Tennessee. He was appointed by Shelby County Mayor Jim Rout to serve on the Shelby County Historical Commission.

Lacey lives in Memphis with his wife of 36 years, Clara Elaine Briscoe-Lacey. He has two adult daughters, Kimberly V. Lacey and Nicole C. Lacey.

TABLE OF CONTENTS

PART I

CHAPTER ONE

THE TRIP TO MEMPHIS

"Do not err, my beloved brethren", **James 1:16**

I t was August and the year was 1984. I had just turned in my grades at Prairie State Community College in Chicago Heights. With the exception of a few students, most had managed to pass the accounting class I taught during the summer session. My teaching responsibilities were also finished at Olive-Harvey College and as for my accounting practice, I had just finished servicing my clients for another month.

With my work responsibilities finished, I was more than ready for a vacation. Vacation usually meant traveling somewhere I had never been before. Since 1975, we had traveled to 48 states, excluding Hawaii and Alaska, and Canada with the family. But, every summer, we managed to get a trip into Memphis. Since I was born in Memphis and left when I was 16, it was good to get back and see family and friends. This trip wouldn't be any different.

"I 'm going to give mother a call and see if she won't change her mind about going to Memphis with us, " I said.

Mother usually accompanied us on vacation, especially on trips to Memphis. Bernice Lewis-Lacey was born in Eads, Tennessee to Jesse Leake-Lewis and Joe Frances Lewis of Eads. Both of her parents were deceased. Her only sibling, a brother lived in Cleveland most of his life. Her husband, Carnegie "Connie" Lacey, was also deceased. He had died in June 1958.

Mother had six children; Connie, Earnest, Joanne, Vivian, Eva and Wayne. All of us live in Chicago, except for Joanne who lives in the Bronx New York, Vivian and Wayne live with Mother on the South Side of Chicago.

"I talked to her earlier this evening and she said she would go next time, " Elaine said. Elaine and I have been married 22 years and we have two daughters, Kimberly and Nicole. Elaine, a striking black woman with a cocoa brown complexion, was born in Memphis too. One of four children of Lillian

Briscoe, Elaine enjoyed trips back to Memphis which allowed her to check on family members. During the time we've been married, she has become very fond of Mother. In fact, they have so much in common she could have easily been mistaken for one of Mother's daughters.

"That's okay. I need to talk to her anyway. We have to leave so early in the morning that it would be best to talk to her tonight," I said, dialing mother's home.

Across town, Bernice was busy hooking a rug. During the1980s, hook rugs became popular and Bernice enjoyed making them to give away as gifts or to put against the door in the wintertime to keep the cold out. Bernice was busily finishing another one as she watched television until the phone rang.

Ring!   Ring!

"Hello, " Bernice said, in an high-pitched voice. Bernice was about five feet tall, with long black hair that had become peppered with gray, a yellowish complexion and high cheek bones.

"Hey there. It's not too late to go with us to Memphis. I've got a few extra dollars if that is what is keeping you from going. We've got plenty of room in the car, " I said.

"No.....not this time. Thanks anyway. Tell 'em all I said hello and the Lord willing, I'll try to get down there next time, " Bernice said in a calm voice.

" Okay.....I just thought you may have changed your mind. Elaine picked up the flowers for the cemetery today and Kim and Nikki have loaded up on their assortment of junk food to eat on the trip," I said laughing.

"I knew they would. I sent Marcell a letter and told her you were coming down there. I know she's going to be disappointed when she doesn't see me, " Bernice said. Bernice and Marcell have been friends for more than forty years. Marcell Gatewood lives on Josephine Street in Orange Mound. Orange Mound is the second oldest black community in America. Married to Lafayette, Sr., Marcell had five children and since his passing in the 1950s, they remained close friends. Only distance separated them now.

"There are so many people to see that we'll probably start making rounds

3

after we check into the hotel tomorrow. I'll probably see Mrs. Gatewood and Ethyl and Suvella soon after we get there," I said. Ethyl Venson and Suvella Horton were sisters and first cousins to Bernice.

"When are you all going out to the cemetery?" Bernice inquired. Gray's Creek Cemetery is in Eads, about 20 miles east of Memphis. It sits a few feet just north of Gray's Creek Baptist Church, which is located at the corner of Airline Road and Highway 64.

"If it's not raining, we'll go to Gray's Creek early Saturday morning. We need to get to Gray's Creek before it gets hot, " I said.

"Don't forget to stop and see Iola. I sent her some money to buy some flowers for the graves, " Bernice said. Iola Brooks was mother's closest first cousin. They had a lot in common. Both had grown up in the rural part of Eads. Iola was the daughter of Eldridge and Addie Lewis. Eldridge and Bernice's father, Joe Frances Lewis, were brothers. Iola was married to Jim Brooks, and they were the parents of an only child, Harold.

"I won't. We'll stop at the cemetery first. I'll stop and see Iola on our way back to Memphis. I just hope she's at home, " I said.

"I'm sure she'll be at home since you'll be stopping early in the morning. You all have a safe trip and be careful. I'll talk to you when you get back, " Bernice said.

"Okay. I'll talk to you then, " I said, hanging up the telephone.

"She's still not coming?" Elaine asked.

" Nope. She said maybe next time, "I replied.

" Daddy? Granny isn't coming with us?" Kim inquired entering the kitchen. Kimberly is the oldest. She enjoyed her grandmother's company on trips.

"Not this time Kim, "I replied.

"Maybe it was because she didn't have any money, " Elaine murmured.

"I don't know and I didn't ask. You know Mother is too proud to ask any-one for anything, " I said.

"Well, it's getting late and I've got some more packing to do, " Elaine said as she walked into the bedroom.

"I'm going to get a shower and hit the bed. I want to be on the road before daybreak, " I said entering the bathroom.

The night passed quickly. Everyone was awakened by the sound of the alarm clock. We dressed and one by one we filed into the bathroom. In the darkness of the morning, the car was loaded. Within a matter of minutes, we were on the Dan Ryan expressway. Our car passed underneath a green and white sign that read, "Memphis South 57".

Five hundred plus miles later, we were in the city of Memphis. It was early afternoon and it was not unlike any other summer day in August — hot. After checking into a hotel, we decided to relax for a while before driving to see cousins Ethyl and Suvella who lived next door to each other on South Parkway.

As we walked up the steps to Ethyl's house, she opened the door.

"For heaven's sake, if it isn't Earnest and his family, " Ethyl said in surprise. Ethyl Belle Horton-Venson was my second cousin. Her deceased mother, Mariah Lewis-Horton was the sister of Joe Frances Lewis, mother's deceased father. Standing about five feet six inches in height, Ethyl had light brown skin and wavy gray hair. Married to R.Q. Venson, one of the first black dentists in Memphis, Ethyl became a well-known civic leader in Memphis championing many causes.

"I'm just fine, " Ethyl replied, as I gave her a hug and kiss on the cheek.

"You all come on in. It's been really hot today. Just look at these gorgeous girls. My my.....they are getting to be big, " Ethyl said smiling.

"Kim is in college now, " Elaine said, proudly with a smile.

"What's the name of your college Kim?," Ethyl inquired.

"The University of Iowa, " Kim said grinning.

"And you are at......?", Ethyl said looking at Nicole.

"I'm at Hyde Park Career Academy, " replied Nicole with a half smile. Nicole is the youngest. Nicole was more reserved and serious.

"Time sure passes fast", Ethyl said with a chuckle.

"Where is Suvella?" I asked.

"Suvella was just here a few minutes before you all came. Let me call her and let her know that you all are here, " Ethyl said picking up the telephone.

After a minute of chitchat with her sister, Ethyl sat down and told us that Suvella was coming right over. Suvella lived upstairs in the house next door to Ethyl.

After about an hour or so of conversing with Ethyl, Suvella never came over. After being on the road since 5 a.m., we were tired and ready to get a bite to eat.

"We're going to be leaving now. It's been a long day for us, " I said as everyone began to walk slowly to the door.

"I don't know what happen to Suvella, " Ethyl said, as we made our way down the short flight of steps onto the sidewalk.

"Did I hear somebody calling my name?", Suvella inquired. A short woman with light brown skin and thinning gray hair, Suvella was a retired nurse. Her son, Quincy, lived in Detroit and was a doctor.

"Earnest, Elaine and the girls were just leaving, because we didn't know where you were, " Ethyl said.

"After I talked to you, another call came in and I just couldn't seem to get off the phone, but I'm here now, " Suvella said hugging Earnest, Elaine, Kim and Nicole.

"Where is Bernice?" Suvella asked surprisingly.

"She didn't make it this time. She sends her regards. Earnest called her last night hoping she would change her mind, " Elaine said smiling.

"I understand. She probably had more important things to do, " Suvella replied.

"Suvella.......aren't these girls growing?", Ethyl inquired.

"They sure are. Beautiful young ladies too, " Suvella replied with a smile.

"Before I forget to ask, can you please tell me why you didn't come down here last month for the family reunion?" Suvella asked with a stern look on her face.

"Reunion! What reunion? I didn't know anything about a reunion," I said surprised.

"We sent out notices and I'm sure we sent one to Bernice, " Suvella said.

"Well......I never got one and Mother never said anything to me about a reunion," I said.

"You really missed out on a nice affair. They gave out information on the family and I bet you didn't know that you have a great, great...... wait a minute, let me count. Two greats for me..... and three for you. You have a great, great, great grandfather that was never a slave, " Suvella said.

"Oh yeah! What was his name?", I asked eagerly.

"Freejoe Harris, "Suvella replied calmly.

"Freejoe Harris!", I replied excitedly.

"That's right. Freejoe Harris, " Ethyl said smiling.

"And he was never a slave, " Suvella repeated.

"Wait a minute. That doesn't make any sense. Where in the world would he get a name like that?" I asked stunned.

"I don't know. That's what they told us, " Suvella said.

"His real name was Joseph Harris and they called him Freejoe, " Ethyl interjected.

"That still doesn't make sense. That name Freejoe implies that he was locked up somewhere. If you were always free, why would you use an adjective like free?," I asked.

"Well, he's buried in Gray's Creek Cemetery, " Suvella said.

"I'm going to the cemetery early tomorrow morning. Do you know where he's buried?", I asked not quite believing this story.

"I have no idea. I was told that he's buried somewhere in the cemetery. That's all I know, " Suvella said.

For a moment, no one said anything.

"I think I know where he's buried, " I murmured

"What! Now aren't you something! A few minutes ago you never heard of the man, didn't know where he was buried, and now all of a sudden you do," Suvella said in a surprised voice.

"I'll be at Gray's Creek at 8:30 a.m. and I'll show you his final resting place, " I said walking toward the car.

"I'll be there. I want to see this, " Suvella said giving everyone a farewell hug.

We all said goodnight. Suvella and Ethyl went into the house as I backed the car out of the driveway.

"Do you really think you know where he's buried?", Elaine asked.

"I know. Don't ask me how I know, but I know," I said.

CHAPTER TWO

GRAY'S CREEK CEMETERY

"Do not err, my beloved brethren", **James 1:16**

I couldn't remember making a trip to Memphis without paying a visit to Gray's Creek Cemetery. For me, it had become part of a routine. It was a way of giving respect to those who had passed on who in some small or large way had made a contribution to the man I had become.

It was early and the heat from the sun at such an early hour was a sure indicator that a hot day was in store for all of us. Suvella and I arrived at the cemetery about the same time.

"You all follow me. I always go down and visit Daddy's and Aunt Jaylone's graves," I said as everyone followed me down near Airline Road.

"Are you sure you know where FreeJoe is buried?", Suvella asked looking straight ahead.

"I'm sure. After we leave here, I'll show you, " I said as Elaine placed flowers on Daddy's and Aunt Jaylone's graves.

After a short visit at Daddy's grave, Carnegie "Connie" Lacey and Jaylone Wright, a great aunt and sister of Bobby Block. Bobby Block was the wife of Lester "Son" Block and sister of Elizabeth Smith, who was the mother of Jesse Leake-Lewis, who was the mother of Bernice Lewis-Lacey. We proceeded in a northwest direction towards the Lewis family plot and suddenly we stopped.

"Let's go over here, " I said pointing in a southwest direction as everyone followed once again.

I walked around to the front of a tall, grayish, thin headstone.

"It says Joseph Harris. Born July 18, 1796, in ?????, Virginia, died July 15, 1875 in Shelby County, Tennessee. I can't make out the county, but it's in Virginia, " I said.

"Well......I'll be! You said you knew where he was buried, " Suvella said gazing down at the writing on the headstone.

"Let me see if I can read the county, " Elaine said feeling with her fingers the writing on the headstone.

"Can you make out the county?" I said standing over the stone.

"I believe it's Goodland County, Virginia. That's what I'm going to write down, " Elaine said.

"Look! Over here! Here is his wife, " I said excitedly.

"Are you sure about that?", Suvella said slowly walking over to view the headstone.

"It says Fanny Harris, the wife of Joseph. She was born on June 24, 1798 and died on April 26, 1865."

"Does it say what county she was born in?" Elaine asked.

"There is no county listed on her headstone, " I said.

"Here is another woman buried next to Fanny and she died on June 3, 1875. Her name is Mary Ford. And it looks like a baby is buried in the grave with her. His name was Alonzo Ford. They must have died in an accident, " I said sadly.

We continued to stand around the headstone of Joseph Harris looking for any clues that would give us information of who he was beyond his name, where he came from and why. But there were no immediate answers for us on that day.

"We are going to stop and see Iola, " I said unlocking the car door.

"Y' all go on. I've got some things I need to take care of. You all come by before you go back to Chicago," Suvella said as she started her car.

Suvella was on her way back to the city when we stopped to see Iola, a short woman who stood about five feet in height with a brown complexion, beautiful black wavy hair and a radiant smile.

As we pulled into the driveway, the chickens began scurrying out of the way. Iola and Jim were farmers and raised chickens and hogs.

"Hey there. How you all doing? You all come on in, " Iola said coming out of the front door smiling.

"You just missed Jim. He might be back before you all leave, " Iola said.

"How are you doing?", I asked giving Iola a hug and a kiss on the cheek.

"We are all doing just fine. No need to complain. Where is Bernice?" Iola asked with a puzzled look on her face.

"She didn't come this time, " Elaine said.

"She didn't! Well, tell her I said hello. Look at them girls. They are really growing. I tell you, " Iola said smiling, as Kim and Nicole smiled back.

"How is Harold and his family?" I asked. Harold was married and has three children.

"They are all doing fine, just fine. Harold was just out here a day or two ago, " Iola said smiling.

"You all going to the cemetery?" Iola asked.

"We just left there. Suvella met us up there. She had to get back to the city, " I said.

"We went by to see Ethyl and Suvella yesterday after we got here," Elaine added, "and Suvella was telling Earnest about a reunion last month that we didn't know anything about."

"Uh huh. The Harris reunion. It was real nice, " Iola said smiling.

"Have you ever heard of a man named Freejoe Harris?" I asked.

"Child no! Not until that reunion last month. The only Joseph I had heard of when I was growing up was grandpa Joseph Lewis, " Iola said.

The door opened and Jim walked in.

"I saw that car with Illinois license plates and I said Earnest or Bernice must be down here, " he said smiling.

"Bernice didn't come this time, " Iola said, lowering her head in a disappointing voice.

"She didn't, " Jim said as the smile disappeared from his face.

"She's not sick, is she?" Jim asked.

"No. I didn't ask her why she wasn't coming", I said.

"Whenever I see Earnest, I expect to see Bernice. Earnest has always been close to Bernice even from the time he was a little boy. I bet the girls miss her not coming too, " Iola said smiling.

"They do, " Elaine said smiling, with Kim and Nicole nodding in agreement.

We departed Iola's house and continued to visit family and friends until we left Memphis to return to Chicago. I began to think more and more about Freejoe. Every thought I had about my great, great, great grandfather was in the form of a question. Why did they call him Freejoe? Why did he come to Tennessee from Virginia? How could I show a connection between him and me? The conversation in the car between Memphis and Chicago centered around Freejoe.

After the car was unloaded and we had settled in for the evening, I called Mother.

"Hello, " Bernice said in a cheery voice.

"It's me. We made it back safe and sound, " I said in a tired voice.

"That's good. How was the trip?", Bernice asked.

"Everything went just fine. It's really hot down there, " I said.

"You can expect that this time of year. How was everybody?", Bernice asked.

"Everybody was fine. They sent their love. They wanted to know where you were," I said.

"Aw yeah, " Bernice said laughing.

"We went out to the cemetery. We saw Iola, Suvella and Ethyl, " I said.

"Did you see Marcell and Ernestine?", she asked.

"We saw Mrs. Gatewood, but we didn't see Ernestine, " I said.

Ernestine Martin was a first cousin of Bernice and the sister of Ethyl Belle Horton-Venson and Suvella Horton.

"Well....you can't see them all, " Bernice said.

"Suvella wanted to know why we didn't come to the family reunion last month, " I said.

"Family reunion! What family reunion?" Bernice asked in a raised voice.

"The Harris family reunion. She said she sent you a letter," I said.

"I don't remember anybody sending me a letter. Oh......wait a minute. I did get a letter. Something about a Harris reunion. I tore the letter up and threw it away. I didn't know anything about any Harrises, " Bernice said calmly.

"You never heard of Freejoe Harris?" I asked.

"Freejoe Harris! No.....never heard of him. You know I left the country when I was small, " she replied.

"Suvella said he was never a slave, but that doesn't make any sense to me. His real name was Joseph Harris, " I said.

"The only Joseph I ever heard of was grandpa Joseph Lewis, " Bernice said.

"Iola said the same thing," I said.

"Alright. You all get some rest. Tell Elaine I'll talk to her tomorrow, " Bernice said.

"Okay. Talk to you then. Goodnight," I said hanging up the telephone.

"Goodnight," Bernice said hanging up the telephone.

"She never heard of Freejoe?" Elaine asked.

"No. She has never heard of him. I'm going to look that county up in the encyclopedia," I said walking towards the living room.

A few minutes passed.

"Did you find it?" Elaine yelled from the bedroom.

"No, not yet", I said as I continued to search.

I walked slowly back to the kitchen.

"Did you find it?" Elaine asked coming out of the bedroom.

"No. There is no county in Virginia named Goodland, " I said dejectedly.

"That was such a long time ago that they may have changed the name, " Elaine said.

"That's possible. I'll call the archives first thing Monday morning, " I said in a lowered voice.

CHAPTER THREE

THE ARCHIVES
"Do not err, my beloved brethren", **James 1:16**

I got up early. It was a Monday morning. This was an important day. I had to find out who this man Freejoe Harris was. My mother and her cousins had never heard of him. It was eight o'clock. It was time to call the archives.

"Good morning. National archives... may I help you, " said a cheerful voice on the other end of the phone.

"Good morning. I'm Earnest Lacey and I was wondering if you could tell me whether a particular county exists or has ever existed, " I said.

"I don't know. What is the name of the county and the state?" the clerk asked.

"Goodland County, Virginia ma'am, " I responded.

"If you will hold, I'll check and see, " she said.

The clerk returned to the phone after a few minutes.

"Hello?"

"Hello. I'm still here, " I said.

"I'm sorry. I can't find a Goodland County, Virginia, " she said.

"Could the name of the county have changed because this man was born in 1796? " I asked.

"If the name of the county has changed, my records would show the new name and the year it was changed. I'm sorry I couldn't be of more help, " she said.

"Oh well. Thank you for your time, " I said. As I began to hang up the phone, I heard shouting through the phone.

"Hello, hello," I said raising the telephone back to my ear.

"I'm glad you didn't hang up. There is a county in Virginia that is close to the name you gave me. Goochland County. It's spelled G.o.o.c.h.l.a.n.d., " she said.

"The headstone was so old and corroded that my wife tried to read it with her fingers as a blind person would, " I said laughing.

"She probably mistook the C and H for a D, " she replied cheerfully.

"Do you have an address for the Goochland County Courthouse?" I asked.

"Yes I do. Clerk, Circuit Court, Goochland County, Virginia 23063, " she replied.

"Thank you very much."

"You're welcome, " replied the clerk, hanging up the telephone.

I didn't realize it at the time, but the clerk at the archives had given me the biggest break in my search for Freejoe. I sent a letter that same day to the clerk at the courthouse in Goochland County, and waited for a reply.

CHAPTER FOUR

DOGWOOD VILLAGE

"Do not err, my beloved brethren", **James 1:16**

T he old people always keep their important papers in a trunk. My mother was no different.

"Hello, " I said.

"It's me," replied Bernice in a cheery voice.

"How are you doing?" I asked calmly.

"I'm doing okay. I was looking through my trunk today and I found a paper that you might want to see. You don't have to come over right away. The next time you come over or come this way, it'll be here, " Bernice said.

A few days later I went over to see Mother.

"I found this in my trunk, " Bernice said, handing a folded document to me.

It was a quit claim deed on some property in Eads, Tennessee. "Virge gave me that deed when he signed his share of Grandpa and Grandma Callie Lewis's property in Eads over to me, " Bernice said. Virge Alexander Lewis was mother's brother.

"I remember. That's the property that Ethyl donated to Dogwood Village, " I said.

"Some of it was sold too, " replied Bernice looking on.

"That's right, " I said in surprise.

"Joseph Harris's name is on the deed. I guess Grandpa and Grandma got it from him, " Bernice said.

"They sure did! That was in 1876, " I said looking at the deed in amazement.

"And all this time I thought that was Grandpa and Grandma Callie's property, " Bernice said with a puzzled look.

"So the property originally belonged to Freejoe Harris, but how did Grandma Callie get the property?," I asked puzzled.

" I guess she must have bought the property from somebody, " Bernice replied as she began to run her fingers through her hair.

After more conversation, I left Mother's house and headed home. Later that evening, Elaine arrived home from work.

"I went over to see Mother today and she showed me a copy of the quit claim deed that Virge signed over to her when they sold the land in Eads, " I said.

"That's the property that we took a tour of back in the 70s. I will never forget that day. Suvella took us all out there and your mother was with us. It was about 10 o'clock in the morning. Suvella told the receptionist that we wanted to take a tour of the place," Elaine said laughing.

"And the receptionist said we would have to come back at 1:30 in the afternoon," I said remembering that day.

"And Suvella told the receptionist that wouldn't be possible because we were from Chicago and would be returning home the next day. When Suvella told the receptionist that we were descendants of Joseph and Callie Lewis.... that receptionist jumped up from that chair as if a spring had broken loose, " Elaine said laughing.

Both Kim and Nikki could be heard laughing loudly from their rooms.

"The marker on the side of the road said that the property was donated by the descendants of Joseph and Callie Lewis. The receptionist just didn't know that the descendants of Joseph and Callie Lewis were of African descent, " I said. Joseph and Callie Lewis were Mother's grandparents and my great grandparents. Callie Lewis was the daughter of Adeline "Lettie" and Jefferson M. Jones. Adeline "Lettie" Jones was Joseph "Freejoe" Harris's daughter.

"After that brief explanation, that receptionist found a tour guide for us in seconds, " Elaine said laughing.

"Do you remember the pears Mother picked off the tree for Kim and Nikki? She was surprised that the tree was still there after all these years. She said it was Grandma Callie's pear tree. Now we find out that the property once belonged to Freejoe, " I said still not quite believing this revelation.

It was Friday and on Fridays I always spent time in the National Archives on Pulaski Road. I had been told by a member of the family that Grandma Callie's mother was a Jones. While looking through the index book for Tennessee in 1860, I found a Jones family living in Fayette County, Tennessee. The head of the household was Jeff Jones. I had found my great, great grandparents. I was excited and rushed home to call mother.

" Mother....have you ever heard of a woman named Caledonia?" I inquired excitedly.

"I can't say that I have, " Bernice replied calmly.

"That's your Grandma Callie. Her real name was Caledonia, " I said.

"I've always heard her referred to as Callie or Callie Frances, " Bernice said.

"The index book had "black family" in brackets. That means that they were free before Lincoln signed The Emancipation Proclamation, " I said.

"That's something, " replied Bernice.

Further research revealed that Jeff Jones was really Jefferson M. Jones and Adeline was given the nickname of Lettie. She was the second oldest daughter of Joseph " Freejoe" and Fanny Harris.

CHAPTER FIVE

A FAT LETTER FROM VIRGINIA

"Do not err, my beloved brethren", **James 1:16**

It was September and Kim had returned to The University of Iowa for another year of study. After Labor Day, Nicole would be back in school at Hyde Park Career Academy. I parked the car like always, in front of the house and began to climb the steps that led to the front door.

"Daddy ! You got a fat letter from Virginia today, " Nicole said excitedly.

"Oh yeah! As soon as I change clothes, I'll open it " I said.

I sat down at the kitchen table and opened the fat letter from Virginia. I read the notes that the clerk in Goochland County had written on my request, which had been returned to me. I began to unfold the documents inside the letter.

"Oh my! This is unbelievable! So that's why they called him Freejoe. He was a slave, " I said giving the papers to Nicole.

"This is just like Alex Haley's story, " Nicole said reading the documents.

When Elaine came home from work she was told about the contents of the fat letter from Virginia. Kim was called at The University of Iowa as well as Ethyl Venson in Memphis. Kim and Ethyl were sent copies of Joseph Harris's Emancipation papers.

Since Joseph Harris was emancipated on September 5, 1832, I decided to look at the first census that he should have appeared in.....the census of 1840. The problem with the 1840 census and all the censuses leading up to 1840, was that they only listed the head of household. I was not able to find him in the 1840 census in Virginia or Tennessee.

I continued my search into the 1850 census in the state of Tennessee. I found Joseph Harris, age 53, living in the ninth civil district of Shelby County with his wife Fanny, age 50, sons John age 16, Cornelius age 14, Alex age 9, and daughters Martha age 5, and Mary age 3. In terms of color, all were listed as mulatto. Joseph was listed as a farmer and his wife was a housewife. His real estate was valued at $1,000. Joseph and Fanny were born in Virginia and all the children were born in Tennessee. Since John was the oldest child living in the household, at the age of 16, and his birth had occurred in Tennessee, I was able to determine that Joseph and Fanny had arrived in Tennessee as early as 1834. Not only that, but in order for Fanny and the children to be listed in the census, they had to be free. The status of the child (slave or free) was predicated on the status of the mother, therefore Fanny had gained her freedom prior to the birth of their son John.

When I checked the 1860 census, I noticed that two additional children had been added to the household and these two daughters were older than any of the children in the 1850 census. I was getting answers, but more questions were coming. Where did these two daughters come from? Some how these two daughters had gained their freedom. Joseph and Fanny's value on their real estate had increased from $1,000. in 1850 to $5,340. in 1860 and the value of their personal estate was $995.

According to the information on Fanny's headstone in Gray's Creek Cemetery, she died in 1865. The 1870 census showed that all the boys had left the house and only the daughters, Martha and Mary remained. But Joseph had another wife and her name was Milly.

My pursuit of Freejoe was interrupted by the death of Virge Lewis, my mother's brother, my uncle and a great, great grandson of Freejoe Harris in November 1984.

Mother and I traveled south to Memphis to bury her brother in Gray's Creek Cemetery. While there, Mother and I took a short walk over to Freejoe's final resting place. This was the first and only time that mother had seen the grave site of her great, great grandfather.

While in Memphis on this sad occasion, I had a conversation with cousin Harold, Iola's son. Harold informed me that another cousin, Jonathan Harris in St. Louis, was doing research on Freejoe too. Jonathan and I exchanged letters several times and had a telephone conversation regarding our findings.

The census records could only provide so much information.

"I think we need to take a trip to Goochland County, " I told Elaine.

"Do you think that's going to help?" Elaine inquired.

"I could pay someone to do the research, but I have no idea if they will do the research and rather than throw money away, I would rather go there and see what I can find, " I said.

It was settled. We went to Goochland County, in August. We searched through records in the Goochland County Courthouse but those efforts produced very little results. I did find that John Harris Sr., Freejoe's father had died in 1843 without leaving a will and the size of the plantation that Joseph was born on was 1,015 acres.

I returned to Chicago disappointed that I hadn't found more than I did. I did gain a lot of satisfaction knowing that my family and I had walked on the same ground that Freejoe had surely walked on over a 100 years before. At least I had seen and knew where Goochland County was and where Joseph had grown up as a child in slavery.

I also learned something else on my trip to Goochland County. Many of the records such as death certificates and birth certificates were not required until the early part of the nineteenth century. Therefore they were not available during the period I was researching. Many records that states kept were destroyed by wars and fires.

I remember on one occasion I inquired about a birth certificate for Joseph in the Goochland County Courthouse and I was told that I would have to go to the department of vital statistics in Richmond.

We drove back to Richmond and went to the department of vital statistics. It was crowded that day. Many parents were seeking birth certificates for their children who were going to school in the fall. When it came my time to be waited on, the clerk told me to go to the archives. I thanked her and walked down the hall towards the elevator. As we walked towards the elevator, my wife informed me the man who had overheard my unusual request was still staring down the hall at me and probably saying to himself, what nut was that?

I continued to write to the courthouse in Goochland County, but the only significant information I received from them was Joseph's emancipation papers. I learned that clerks in the courthouse don't usually search their records for information on any particular family. They just don't have the time.

Since there were very few places I could learn how to research genealogy, I was slowly earning my degree through the corridors of hard knocks and disappointments were just part of the process.

Somehow I knew their was a lot of information on Freejoe. I couldn't stop my search now if I wanted to. There was a driving force within me to find more information. I was beginning to change. My priorities were changing. My interest in sports was being pushed aside to make room for genealogy. In my conversations at the archives on Fridays, I began to see that the information I was gathering was coming just the opposite of the way others were gathering their information.

On our return to Chicago from Goochland County, it was the time of year that we usually went to the farms in the southern suburbs of Chicago to pack the freezer with vegetables for the winter. Mother always went with us. This trip was no exception. As we were leaving one of the farms, I glanced into the rear view mirror.

"What's wrong Mother? " I inquired as Elaine turned around.

"I don't know. I haven't been able to keep very much on my stomach, " she replied.

"I think we should go home now, " I said concerned.

"No....I'll be all right. Let's go on to the last farm", Bernice said calmly.

"How long has this been going on ?" Elaine asked.

"Oh...about a week I guess, " Bernice said.

"Does it hurt?" Elaine inquired.

"No, it doesn't hurt. I just can't keep anything down, " Bernice said quietly.

"Have you been to the doctor?" I asked continuing to drive.

"No. Not yet. You know I don't care for doctors, " Bernice replied.

"After we take you home, I'll call you and give you Dr. London's telephone number. You should go and see him, " I said.

After we left the farms, we took Mother to her house and continued on home. I didn't know it at the time, but another change had started in my life.

Mother's condition seem to subside. I went by to see her one day to share with her something that was on my mind

"I don't know what it is, but this research I'm doing on Freejoe Harris is taking up more and more of my time, " I said calmly.

"I don't know what to tell you. It's six of you and for some reason you have always had a deep interest in this family. As we get older we tend to start caring more about who the old heads were, but you were like that as a little fellow, " Bernice said laughing.

"I feel like I'm being pulled away from here by some kind of force. I'm losing some of my business accounts. When the economy sours, we always catch it first. It's the only time we are first in line. We don't know whether the politicians in Springfield will fund the program at Olive-Harvey College next year or not, " I said.

"Nothing good ever happens when the Republicans get in office, " Bernice said shaking her head.

"The police and fire calls are up in the neighborhood and that's a sign that the community is starting to deteriorate. I have a real concern for Elaine, Kim, and Nikki's safety. I talked to Ms. Reese over at the school and she said the children moving into the community are coming in under grade level. That's another bad sign, " I said.

"A lot of that is going on everywhere. Evidently you've been doing a lot of thinking, " Bernice said pulling on her hair.

"Yes I have. I've come to the conclusion that I have no other choice than to move. I mean out of the state, " I said.

"Have you talked to Elaine about this?" Bernice inquired.

"Not yet. I will tonight, " I said.

"Do you have any idea where you are going to move to? " Bernice asked.

"It's going to be South. Industry and jobs are moving South. People have to go where the work is going. San Antonio and Memphis are possibilities. Right now I don't know which one it will be, " I said.

"I tell you what. When you put your house up for sale, I'm putting this one up because I'll be moving too," Bernice said calmly.

That evening a discussion on the possibility of moving was discussed.

"How was your mother?" Elaine asked as she began cooking dinner.

"She said she was feeling better, " I said.

"Is she still working on Virge's affairs?" inquired Elaine.

"Yes...but right now she's waiting on the attorneys, " I said.

"Anyway, Mother and I had a long talk about how the neighborhood is changing. I told her I felt like I'm being pulled away from Chicago and how we might have to move, " I said.

"Move! Don't you think I should have some say so in whether we move, " Elaine said loudly.

"That depends on whether you see what I see. Jobs are leaving the city. The number of clients I have are decreasing. Funding in Springfield is questionable every school year. This is not a time to hold a debate. It seems to me that some hard and fast decisions have to be made concerning the welfare of this family and as the head of this family, I have to fulfill my responsibility, " I said.

"We could move to the suburbs, " Elaine said in disgust.

"We could, but I would have to give up my job at Olive-Harvey College because in order to work in the City College system, you must live in the city, " I said.

"The only answer I see is to move South, out of the state. That's where industry and jobs are going right now. You have to go where the jobs are going," I said calmly.

"Where in the south?" Elaine asked.

"I don't know yet. San Antonio or Memphis. Helen lives in San Antonio and we both have family in Memphis, " I said. Helen was Elaine's first cousin and John Seymore was her husband.

"You said you talked to your Mother about this. What did she say?" Elaine asked.

"She said when we put this house up for sale, she's going to put hers up too.,"

I said.

I continued to visit the archives on Fridays. We went to Mother's for Thanksgiving and she came to our house for Christmas. After mother left for home on Christmas Day, I was deeply concerned.

"Mother didn't hardly eat anything, " I said sadly.

"I know. She said she wasn't hungry. I noticed something else about her too, " Elaine said.

"You don't have to tell me. She has lost a lot of weight, " I said.

CHAPTER SIX

MOTHER'S DEATH

"Do not err, my beloved brethren", **James 1:16**

I didn't know what to think anymore. Mother had been diagnosed with cancer. My daily routine had changed. I had to take mother for treatments on a daily basis. It was difficult to talk to Mother about those ancestors that had passed on. We were in the car headed south on the Dan Ryan expressway.

"I had a dream last night and something in my stomach burst, " Bernice said softly gazing out of the window.

I didn't know how to respond to Mother's comments so I remained silent.

"The cancer has spread, " Bernice said calmly.

"Mother I'm sorry. I wish there was something I could do for you, " I replied.

"There is nothing you can do. There is nothing anyone can do. I knew a long time ago that one day I would have to die, " Bernice said with a straight face.

Silence invaded the car. Only the passing cars and the L trains along the Dan Ryan expressway could be heard. I marveled at this lady sitting next to me. I felt proud and fortunate that she was my Mother. Her fate had been sealed and she spoke of death in such a calm manner. I knew then that she had made peace with the Lord. She was ready to cross that river that we all must cross one day.

I had taken Mother for another one of her treatments at Rush Presbyterian Hospital and we were on the Dan Ryan expressway, on our way back to her home on Yale.

"I'm going to Memphis Mother, " I said suddenly.

Mother didn't reply right away. I felt her hand touch mine as I looked straight ahead, with one hand on the steering wheel and the other on the seat between us.

"You go. Go to Memphis. You're always helping people, " Bernice said in an encouraging way, looking straight ahead.

"I'm sorry you won't be able to go with us, " I said softly.

"Some things just can't be helped, " Bernice said looking straight ahead.

The days passed and mother continued to lose weight and strength.

On April 14, 1986, Bernice Earnestine Lewis-Lacey passed away. The widow of Carnegie "Connie" Lacey, mother of Connie Jr., Earnest, Joanne, Vivian, Eva Rean and Wayne. Mother was laid to rest in Gray's Creek Cemetery.

Over the next few months, the search for Freejoe was put on hold while I worked on her and Virge's estates.

In the meantime, we all had received notices of the Harris family reunion scheduled for the July 4th weekend in St. Louis.

Family members including Joe Branch and Charlie Morris Sr. in Memphis and Jonathan Harris and Sylvia Small in St. Louis, had done some family research. Sylvia came to Chicago prior to the reunion to discuss our individual findings. At this point, the conclusion was that I had found more information than they had.

At the family reunion in July 1986, someone had secured and made copies of the will of Joseph " Freejoe" Harris that had been filed in 1875 in the Shelby County Courthouse. This narrative portion of the will stated who would get what and how much.

CHAPTER SEVEN

HOUSE HUNTING IN MEMPHIS

"Do not err, my beloved brethren", **James 1:16**

During the remaining months of 1986 I was able to finalize the estates of my uncle, and my mother. Instead of focusing more attention on my research, I was preoccupied with the move to Memphis. Kim would be graduating from the University of Iowa in May and Nicole was narrowing her choice of colleges.

"Well Daddy, it looks like I'll be attending Culver-Stockton College in Canton, Missouri. They are offering me a full academic scholarship," Nicole said smiling.

"Are you sure you want to go there? You don't have to accept just because it will save me money, " I replied.

"I worked hard at Hyde Park for four years and I feel I deserve a scholarship. Besides they offer a journalism major, " Nicole said.

"I'm sure your mother will be glad to hear the news when she gets home. She applied for a scholarship on her job for you. They offer a scholarship for students of employees, " I said.

"I know. Ma told me, " Nicole replied.

"Well, congratulations!" I said with a big smile.

"Thanks. I'll tell Kim on the weekend when we call her, " Nicole said smiling.

Nicole informed her mother of the scholarship offer when she arrived from work.

"Nicole told me about her scholarship offer. That's nice. I hope she doesn't feel she has to take it because of us, " Elaine said.

"I mentioned that to her. She said she wants to major in journalism and she's going to take their offer, " I said.

"I should be hearing something pretty soon at work about the scholarship, " Elaine said.

"It looks more and more like we 're headed for Memphis, " I said smiling.

"You get copies of the Sunday edition of The Commercial Appeal every Tuesday and you haven't made any contacts for a job or house, " Elaine said dejectedly.

"I know. I'm thinking about opening an accounting practice in Memphis, " I said.

"That takes time. Look at how long it took here, " Elaine said.

"It does take time. One of my students has been talking to me about selling investments. I could combine that with my accounting. I told her that I might move to Memphis, " I said.

"What about a place to stay in Memphis? " Elaine said.

"I would like to get a new house in a nice neighborhood. I've been thinking about calling Keith. You remember Keith Harris. I asked him to find something for his old baseball coach. He lives in Bartlett, Tennessee, " I replied.

"Have you thought about what time of the year we would go down there to start house hunting?" Elaine asked.

"Spring break seems like a good time. Kim and Nikki will be on spring break, " I said.

Several calls were made to Keith and he was able to get an appointment with the real estate agent that sold him his house. We went out to see several houses. We weren't please with any of them. We returned to our hotel. It was early afternoon.

The phone rang and it was Keith on the other end.

Keith was almost six feet tall. He had played on my baseball team during the summer on the south side of Chicago at Gately Stadium. I had known Keith since he was 12 years old. I was very proud of him and his accomplishments. I assisted him in entering Friends University in Wichita, Kansas. He later transferred to and graduated from Wichita State University in Wichita. Keith had been placed in a management program by Jiffy Lube and was sent to Memphis. While in Wichita, Keith also met his wife Debbie.

"Hello, Keith. How are you?", I asked.

"I'm fine. I just called to see how things went today, " Keith replied in a cheery voice.

"Not too good. She didn't show us anything decent, " I said sadly.

"Oh man. I thought she was pretty good. I've got to take the boys to base-ball practice. Can you meet me at Yale and Bartlett Boulevard around six?" Keith asked.

"Sure. We'll get something to eat and meet you there, " I replied.

"You can't miss it. Central Church North is on the corner, " Keith said.

"See you there, " I said hanging up the phone.

"Keith wants us to meet him at Yale and Bartlett Blvd. We'll eat early so we won't be late, " I said excitedly.

We met Keith and walked along Yale looking at new houses.

"There are some nice houses over here. I don't know why she didn't bring you all over here, " Keith said smiling.

We continued to walk down one side of Yale and then on the other side of the street. We still hadn't found a house that we liked. It was getting dark. I was tired and disappointment was being to set in.

"Daddy, there is a man sitting in a house across the street, " Nikki said pointing in the direction of the house.

"Daddy, do you want to go over there?" Kim asked quietly.

"No...I'm disgusted and tired," I said.

"We might as well have a look. One more stop won't hurt, " Elaine said.

"I know how you feel Mr. Lacey, " Keith said as we crossed the street.

We walked into the model home and waited our turn.

"How are you folks this evening?," the salesman asked smiling.

"Just tired. We are from Chicago, " Elaine said half smiling.

"Disgusted is a better word, " I said.

The salesman let out a loud laugh.

"Maybe I can help you folks. I'm Joe Escue, " Joe said extending his hand. Joe was short and a little on the heavy side. He was pleasant with a friendly attitude that matched his bright smile.

"I'm Earnest Lacey and this is my wife Elaine, my daughters Kimberly and Nicole. This is a friend of the family, Keith Harris, and he lives here, " I said extending my hand.

That next day we finally found a house we liked.

"I've got this house in another subdivision at a cheaper price. We've already started building on it and if you like it, I'll sell it to you. It's in Forest Lakes North. It's too dark this evening, but if you come by here tomorrow morning at 9, I'll take you over there, " Joe said.

We met Joe the following morning and agreed to purchase the house on Allendale Drive. It was early in the afternoon when we completed the paper work. We departed Memphis the following day for Chicago.

CHAPTER EIGHT

COTTAGE GROVE HEIGHTS

"Do not err, my beloved brethren", **James 1:16**

I was washing my car in front of the house when one of my neighbors came out of his house.

"Hey.....Earnie, " Willie said walking towards me. Willie Robinson was of medium build with curly black hair. He and his family had lived in the neighborhood for almost 20 years. We were close neighbors.

"Willie! How's it going?" I asked.

"Pretty good. No complaints. I didn't see you all around on the weekend. I told Eva and Peaches that you all must be out of town, " Willie said. Eva Brown and Peaches (Mamie Scott) were Willie's sisters-in-law. They were the sisters of Willie's deceased wife, Lucille "Nan" Robinson.

"We went to Memphis, " I said applying soapy water to the car.

"I know the weather was nice down there. It's not too hot this time of year. Mrs. Lacey died about this time last year. Time flies. Nan and Mrs. Lacey died in the same year. It will be a year in September for Nan." Willie said.

"I'm moving Willie, " I said.

"I don't think I heard you, " Willie said moving closer with a hand to his ear.

"I'm moving," I said.

"That's what I thought you said. You're going back to Memphis, Freejoe Country. You going to put your Bulls, Cubs and Bears down, " Willie said smiling.

"Not really. I've been hanging with them too long now to put them down. You know I'll always be a Chicago sports fan. I'll just have to watch them from a distance now, and with cable I won't be far away, " I said grinning.

"I wish you the best. When do you think you'll leave?" Willie asked.

"I don't know. We are having a house built and we have to sell this one," I replied.

"Well, I'll be talking to you before you leave, " Willie said, slowly walking away.

"Okay. That will be a while, " I said in a loud voice.

The house on Woodlawn was put up for sale.

"What are we going to do about the Harris reunion in Chicago next year?" Elaine asked.

"I'll see if someone else will chair the effort and if no one can, we'll have to do it from Memphis, " I said.

When Wilks Brooks, Geneva Archer, Bernice Thomas and Flossie Wilson met for the reunion meeting, they were informed of our plans to move to Memphis. It was decided that I would continue to chair the reunion committee from Memphis.

One of my former students at Prairie State Community College, Bobby King, introduced me to Darwin Yarbrough of Waddell and Reed Financial Services. Yarbrough was the office manager. I agreed to work for them on a part-time basis out of their Park Forest office until I moved to Memphis. At that time, I would transfer to the Waddell and Reed office in Memphis.

By showing that I had employment, it would be easier to buy a new home in Memphis. I would also have a base of financial clients.

"I want to take this opportunity to congratulate Earnest on being named salesman of the month for the month of May " Yarbrough said smiling.

"Thank you very much. I really appreciate the opportunity that you have given me, " I said grinning.

"You see, you see. I told you that you would be good at this, " Bobby said smiling.

"Let me just say something else about Earnest. It is truly amazing what he has accomplished. He beat out full time salesmen in order to win this award. Are you sure I can't change your mind about moving to Memphis?" Yarbrough asked smiling.

"No. I'm afraid not, " I said.

Within weeks a buyer was found for the house. By now the word had spread up and down the block that the Laceys were moving.

"Elaine .....when Willie told me that you all were moving, I couldn't believe it, " Eva Brown said with a straight face.

"And Earnest.....I'm just so angry with you I don't know what to do, " Peaches said sadly.

"What can I say Peaches, " I said smiling with arms wide open.

"I'm going to miss my girls, " Eva said.

"You know I will too, " Peaches said.

The weeks passed quickly. A possible closing date on the house was given for August. I finished my teaching assignments at Prairie State College and Olive-Harvey City College. I said my last good byes.

On our last Sunday in Chicago, the Reverend Jeremiah A. Wright Jr., pastor of Trinity United Church of Christ summoned my family and I to the alter for a special prayer and blessing. It was another round of good byes.

It was Friday now and it had rained hard most of the day. Elaine and I had difficulty finding the location for the closing of the house. After the closing ,we returned to the house we had called home for twenty years. The movers had came and gone. The house was empty. Elaine, Kimberly, Nicole and I took our last walk through the empty house. Not a word was spoken. Each of us privatized our thoughts.

We drove to a motel to spend the night. We departed the Chicago area the following morning. I had lived in Chicago for 32 years, but the time had come to say goodbye.....to family and friends, and all that I had become accustomed to. We were Memphis bound.

CHAPTER NINE

OUR NEW HOME

" Do Not err, my beloved brethren", **James 1:16**

As the old folks use to say, Memphis was hotter than Cooter Brown. It was Saturday, August 18, 1987. We arrived at our new house and unloaded the car. The movers hadn't arrived yet. They had promised to contact our real estate agent when they arrived in town, so our agent could show them how to find the house.

We didn't have a telephone. It was 1:30 p.m. It was getting late and there was no sign of the movers. We went to dinner and came back and still there was no sign of the movers. It was almost 9 p.m. There was a ring at the door.

"That's probably them now, " Elaine said frowning.

"No....its Mr. Escue, " I said opening the door.

"Mr. Escue! Come on in! " I said holding open the door.

"Earnest, I've got some bad news for you, " Joe said stepping inside the door.

"I just got a call from your movers. Their truck broke down in New Madrid, Missouri. They said they won't get here until between noon and one tomorrow, " Joe said sadly.

"We'll be all right. Thanks Joe. I'm sorry to put you to all this trouble. We'll get a hotel for the night, " I said.

"I wish I had better news for you, " Joe said as he left.

We got into the car and began to look for a hotel to spend the night. Everything was booked up so we returned to our house and spent the first night sleeping on the floor. The movers arrived the following day, a Sunday.

Before we could begin to settle into our new home, we had to drive Nicole to Canton, Missouri so she could start classes at Culver-Stockton College.

On my initial day of work at Waddell and Reed Financial Services, I was introduced to the staff.

"I'd been told that a fellow was transferring here from Chicago or Detroit. I'm pleased to meet you. I'm Matthew Gray, " Matthew said. Matthew was heavy set. He seemed friendly and eager to talk.

"I'm pleased to meet you Mr. Gray. I'm Earnest Lacey out of Chicago, " I said smiling.

"Oh Chicago! I wasn't sure if it was Chicago or Detroit and if you want to know the truth, I think everybody thought you were going to be a white man. Not too many of our people are in this line of business. What brings you to Memphis,? " Matthew asked.

I wasn't sure how I was going to answer Matthew's question. If I told him I was sent by God he would think I was crazy. Before I could answer Matthew's question, he fired off another one.

"Do you have family here? " Matthew asked waiting for answers.

"I sure do. I was born here. My mother was a Lewis and she grew up in Eads. I'm related to Ethyl Venson, Suvella Horton, Ernestine Martin, Iola Brooks, Harold Brooks and Joe Branch, just to name a few," I said smiling.

Matthew just listened as I rattled off the names.

"You know...you're related to me too. Those are my cousins, " Matthew said calmly with a smile.

"I'm not surprised. Mother said we were related to the Grays."

It took more than two months for my investment license to be transferred to Tennessee. By now the bottom had dropped out of the stock market. We had to fall back on our reserves. There were times when I didn't know how we would make it financially, but with the grace of God we did.

Someone or something wanted to make sure I didn't return to Chicago. As an accountant, I had done taxes for more than 20 years. I never had a year in taxes in Chicago like the first one I had in Memphis. I had been told that whites wouldn't patronize me and black folks didn't have any money to invest. I had to find out for myself. Over 95 percent of my tax clients were white and I found some black folks that had money to invest.

This financial success wasn't enough to sustain my family and I over the long haul so I began to look for employment opportunities elsewhere.

It wasn't long before I became a business consultant for The Tennessee Small Business Development Center. This job gave me an opportunity to get back to my family research.

The Harris family reunion that was scheduled for Chicago took place as scheduled. It felt strange visiting a place that I once called home for 32 years. The gathering wasn't as large as had been anticipated but there were enough of us to speculate on various aspects of the life of Joseph "Freejoe" Harris.

We returned to Memphis and I settled into my new job. I had been at the Center now for a little over five months.

An article appeared in The Commercial Appeal that caught my eye. "Old Building Might Be Moved, Structure May Be From Late 1820s." I began to read the article and it said, "Some say it later was a stagecoach stop called Freejoe's, run by a slave named Joe, who earned his freedom before the Civil War." The article went on to say that Freejoe's was one of the most popular stagecoach stops because of good food. The brick structure was on Highway 64. I called The Commercial Appeal and asked for the writer of the article.

"This is John Knott, " John said in a heavy voice.

"Hello John. I'm Earnest Lacey. I called about the article you wrote the other day concerning the old brick structure on Highway 64, " I said.

"Oh yes. What can I help you with?" John asked.

"I just want to make some corrections and some additions to your article. First of all the man you referred to in the article was not a slave. He was emancipated on September 5, 1832 in Goochland County, Virginia. His real name was Joseph Harris and the plantation in Virginia where he was born, was owned by his father, John Harris Sr., a white man. The slaves gave him the nickname "Freejoe". The building that people believe was his Inn, was not. The Inn was located near the stagecoach stop at Airline Road where

Gray's Creek Baptist Church is located, " I said in an authoritative voice.

"You seem to know a lot about this man. Who are you? " John asked.

"I'm Freejoe's great, great, great, grandson, " I replied.

"Where are you now? ", John asked.

"320 South Dudley,"

"I'll be there in about fifteen minutes, " John said.

Within minutes John was at the office.

"I'm John Knott. Is that your car outside? The one with the Freejoe license plate?" John asked extending his hand.

"Yes it is. There is one on the front from the state of Illinois. I recently moved here from Chicago, " I said shaking his hand.

"Before I leave I would like to take a picture of you and the car, " John said.

John and I chatted about the old brick structure on Highway 64 and Freejoe Harris. John took a picture of me and the car and left.

On Thursday December 29, 1988, another article entitled " Descendant sheds some new light on former slave" appeared in The Commercial Appeal, written by John Knott.

Subsequent articles were written on the brick structure that was eventually moved to Germantown, Tennessee. It's called The John Gray house. I chuckle now at how Freejoe's name got mixed up in the brick structure that use to occupy 10133 Highway 64. Some said it was the place where he had his Inn. Some said he did not own the property. They are wrong and right on both counts. But the structure wasn't built in the 1820s either. Just how did Freejoe's name get mixed up in this building in the first place? It's all rather simple. He built the brick structure. Joseph" Freejoe" Harris was a master builder.

CHAPTER TEN

MOUND BAYOU, MISSISSIPPI

"Do not err, my beloved brethren", **James 1:16**

M elvin McCoy arrived at the Tennessee Small Business Development Center office on Dudley shortly after 8 a.m.

"This is a lovely day to take a trip. I'm glad it's not raining, " I said.

"Me too, " Melvin said getting into the car. Melvin was about six feet tall. He had invented an apparatus that was designed for use by outdoors men and military foot soldiers. He was also very articulate.

"It's been a while since I've been to Mississippi, " I said with a chuckle.

"I was really lucky to find this company. At one time they were located in Arlington, Tennessee and evidently Bill Richardson, the owner, felt that the opportunities were greater in Mound Bayou, " Melvin said.

"So this company moved from Arlington. I was told that my great, great, great, grandfather, "FreeJoe" Harris had a grandson that was one of the founders of Mound Bayou, " I said.

"That's interesting. By the way, how is your overall research going?" Melvin asked.

"It's coming along. A little bit here and there," I replied.

"When was your great, great, great grandfather born?" Melvin asked.

"1796 in Goochland County, Virginia during the administration of President George Washington, " I said.

"Whoa! That was a long time ago, " Melvin said with a short laugh.

We finally arrived at The Mohawk Cycle Corporation in Mound Bayou. We were given a tour of the company.

"Bill has a contract with a major retailer, " Melvin said gleefully

"Yes we do, " Bill said proudly as he continued to show us around his plant.

" I want you to meet my wife Juanita, " Bill said, as we entered her office. Juanita had a smile that lit up the room.

"This is Mr. McCoy. He is the fellow that I was telling you about that invented the M.U.L.E., " Bill said.

"And this is... Bill said unable to remember my name.

"Mr. Lacey. He is a business consultant with the Tennessee Small Business Development Center in Memphis, " Melvin said interrupting.

"I'm pleased to meet you Mrs. Richardson. I understand you all are from Arlington. I have relatives who live in Arlington, " I said smiling.

"I'm please to meet you. I really miss home. I go back as often as I can. So you have relatives in Arlington? That's such a small place I'm sure Bill and I probably know your relatives, " Juanita said smiling.

"Some of them live in Eads. Iola Brooks and Florence Branch, " I said proudly.

"Earnest is researching his family. What was your great, great, great, grand-father's name?" Melvin asked.

"Freejoe Harris, " I said.

"Did you say Harris? " Juanita asked in a surprised tone.

"Yes I did. Joseph "Freejoe" Harris."

"I was Juanita Branch before I married Bill, " Juanita said with a smile.

"Branch! You and I are related, " I said laughing.

"We are?" Juanita asked laughing.

"Freejoe had a daughter named Martha and she married George Branch. He also had a daughter named Adeline that they called Lettie. Lettie married Jefferson M. Jones and that union produced a daughter named Callie Frances that married Joseph Lewis. They had a son named Joe. Joe married Jessie

Leake and they had a son name Virge and a daughter named Bernice. Bernice married Carnegie" Connie" Lacey and that union produced six children including me, " I said.

"Man! He sure knows how it all connects up, " Bill said.

We finished our business at The Mohawk Cycle Corporation.

"Bill, I'll get in touch with you and we will iron out the details. Earnest and I are going to make a stop at the Mayor's office. Earnest wants to check on some of his ancestors while he's here, " Melvin said.

"You have relatives working for Mayor Lucas?" Bill asked.

"No. Freejoe had a grandson named Peter. He was a preacher and rumor has it that he was one of the founders of Mound Bayou. I want to see if they have a list of the founders, " I said.

"I wish you luck and come back to see us, " Bill said.

We journeyed a short distance to The Mayor's office. I was given a list of the founders of Mound Bayou, the largest Negro town in America.

"Did you find what you were looking for?" Melvin asked.

"I sure did. Peter Harris, the grandson of Freejoe Harris, and the son of James and William Harris, the grandson of Freejoe Harris, and the son of Peter were both founders of Mound Bayou, Mississippi. William and Peter were cousins and preachers," I replied.

The clerk gave me a copy of the Mound Bayou centennial celebration booklet. Melvin and I departed Mound Bayou for Memphis. The search for Freejoe was full of surprises.

CHAPTER ELEVEN

A COMMUNITY BLESSING

"Do not err, my beloved brethren", **James 1 :16**

We had finished our work in the cemetery and stopped to visit with Iola on our way back to the city.

"Earnest, did you ever talk to Mr. Johnson about some of those things that you are looking for?" Iola asked.

"No, I haven't yet ,"I replied

I was looking for someone who could give me some oral history on Joseph "FreeJoe" Harris.

"Earnest.... Elaine... how are you, ?" Harold asked.

"We're doing just fine. We just left the cemetery, " I said.

"I just got here too. I've got a few things around here to patch up for Mama. Earnest, I just heard Mama refer you to Mr. Johnson. You should also talk to Charlie Harris. If I'm not mistaken, Charlie Harris is about the oldest Harris living out here. He's been around a long time too, " Harold said.

"I'll do just that. I appreciate the suggestion, " I said smiling.

"I don't believe I have Charlie's telephone number, but I've got Mr. Johnson's, " Iola said, getting up from her chair to go into the house. Iola wasn't gone long before she returned with the phone number.

"You'll find him at home anytime of the day, " Iola said smiling.

"Earnest......let me tell you about Mr. Johnson. He's in his nineties and his mind is sharp. He can remember things that happened 70 years ago as if they happened yesterday, " Harold said with a smile. A few days later, I called Robert Johnson and we agreed on a time and day that I would come to the house. I had prepared a list of questions and I had a pen, pad and tape recorder.

"Mr. Johnson.....I'm Earnest Lacey, " I said smiling.

"I'm pleased to meet you, " he replied opening the door. He was of medium build, with gray hair that was cut low, and he moved about slowly.

I inquired about an outlet for my tape recorder and Mr. Johnson pointed to an outlet on a nearby wall.

"Have a seat, " Mr. Johnson said pointing.

"Thank you. As I told you on the phone, Iola Brooks told me that whatever I needed to know about Gray's Creek Baptist Church and the people in Eads, you could tell me, " I said laughing.

"Well.....I don't know about that. I'll do my best, " Mr. Johnson said, slowly choosing his answer.

"If you don't mind me asking, how old are you ?" I asked.

"I don't mind. If the good Lord is willing, I'll be 98 years old on March 15 next year, " Mr. Johnson said proudly.

"That is truly amazing. I'm just glad that God has allowed our paths to cross. I would like to play a game with you. It's called the name game, " I said.

"I don't know that game, " Mr. Johnson said with a slight smile.

"It's an easy game to play. I'll give you a name and you tell me what you know or have heard about that person, " I said.

Mr. Johnson just sat silently as I began to give him names.

"What can you tell me about Joseph Lewis? He was my great grandfather, " I said.

"He died in 19 and 18. He was a deacon at Gray's Creek Church when he died. We all called him Uncle Joe, " Mr. Johnson said.

"He had a son named Joe. He was my grandfather and he was killed, " I said.

"I remember little Joe very well. He was married to a woman named Jessie. She was a nice looking woman. I remember when he brought her to the

43

church festival. None of us had ever seen her before. Next thing we know, they done got married. They had two little children. Then little Joe got shot to death, " Mr. Johnson said sadly.

"Whatever happened to his wife?" I asked.

"I don't rightly know what happened to Miss. Jessie, " he replied.

"My mother said she died in Pecan Point, Arkansas. Where ever that is. " I said.

"I don't know about that. I don't know what happen to Miss. Jessie. Miss. Jaylone Wright and her husband John Wright raised the children, " Mr. Johnson said rubbing his head.

"Those two children were my uncle and mother, Virge and Bernice," I said.

"Shonuff! I didn't know what ever happened to those children, " he said.

"What do you know about a man named Joseph Harris? They called him Freejoe, " I asked.

Mr. Johnson thought for a few seconds and moved forward in his seat.

"He was the first pastor of Gray's Creek Baptist Church, " he said.

"What else can you tell me about him,?" I asked.

"I wasn't around when he was around, " he replied.

"I know, but what did you hear that others had to say about him,? " I asked.

"If you were hungry, he fed you. If you didn't have any clothes, he would cloth you. If you didn't have a place to stay, he would find a place. If you had a disagreement with a neighbor, he would bring you together, listen to both sides and make a ruling and he expected you to obey his ruling, " Mr. Johnson said, as chills ran up and down my spine.

"Sounds like Freejoe was the messiah of Eads. What can you tell me about Gray's Creek Missionary Baptist Church?", I asked.

"Freejoe was the first pastor of Gray's Creek. That was in February of 18 and 43, " he said.

"I understand the church was once a white church. What was the name of it when the whites had it?" I asked.

"When the whites had it, it was a Camelot church, " Mr. Johnson said.

"Camelot church,?" I said, not knowing at the time that Mr. Johnson meant Campbellite church.

We discussed a number of ministers that succeeded Freejoe Harris as pastor of Gray's Creek Baptist Church.

"Freejoe Harris had several grandchildren that became ministers. One of them was Peter Harris. What can you tell me about him,?" I said.

"I remember Peter Harris. He was a traveling preacher. He would go around and organize churches. Once he got them organized, he would turn them over to another preacher. They use to call him snake-eyed Pete because he had slanted eyes, " he said.

"Freejoe had a daughter name Sucky. Her real name was Susan, " I said.

Mr. Johnson seemed puzzled for a moment.

"Oh yes. She was an old woman. She use to cook for the Bragg family, " he said.

"I want to thank you for all this information. I'm really glad that you are here. I believe that this is all a part of God's plan, " I said.

"I'm just glad I could help in some way. Let me to do what I can, while I can, when I can, If I can, as long as it is right, " Mr. Johnson said, as I placed some money in his hand.

"You don't have to do that, " he said looking me in the face.

"I know. I just want you to buy yourself something, " I said smiling .

Mr. Johnson and I walked out on the porch and he insisted on giving me a tour of his large garden of okra, tomatoes, butter beans and a few other plants.

Mr. Johnson is the historian and elder deacon of Gray's Creek Baptist Church in Eads. He is a blessing to his community. His mind is as sharp today as it was at the turn of the century. As of this writing, Mr. Robert Johnson is 101 years old and counting.

Note: On Friday February 13, 1998, Brother Robert E. Johnson II, went home to be with the Lord. He was thirty days away from his 102nd birthday.

CHAPTER TWELVE

MED WEEK MEETING

"Do not err, my beloved brethren", **James 1:16**

I was running late for a minority enterprise development (Med) week meeting at The Days Inn in downtown Memphis. The meeting was already in session, so I found the first available chair, and sat down. Gary Rowe, the minority Small Business Development Director had the floor. Unknowingly at the time, I had sat next to Frank Banks. The meeting was now over.

"Hello Frank, It's good to see you again, " I said smiling.

"Earnest....how are you doing?" Frank asked. I had known Frank for a long time. We had met back in Chicago when Frank came to live with his brother Floyd, after graduating from Xavier University in New Orleans.

"I'm fine. I got tied up with a client this morning and the session ran a little longer than I expected. How are you doing?" I asked.

"I'm doing okay. Things are going along well," he said.

"How is Floyd doing,?"I asked.

"Floyd is fine. He was just down here. You know he brings his school down here every other year to play Melrose High School and every other year Melrose goes to Chicago to play Dunbar High School, " Frank replied.

"That's great. That's a wonderful thing that Floyd is doing. The next time he comes down, let me know. I haven't seen him in years, " I said.

"How is your research coming,?" Frank asked.

"It's coming along. I've been asked to talk to a fellow by the name of Arthur Webb. Trouble is......I don't know where to find him, " I said laughing.

Frank laughed.

"He works in my office. He's working on a calendar that highlights the accomplishments of African-Americans in West Tennessee," he said.

"Tell him not to forget Freejoe, " I said smiling.

"That's right. He's your great, great....., " he said pausing.

"Three greats," I said finishing his sentence.

"I'll tell him, " Frank said walking away.

It was late in the afternoon of the same day when I got a call at the office.

"Lacey speaking."

"Lacey....Arthur Webb. What would you say if I told you that Joe and Fanny Harris were the first couple of color in Shelby County to get a marriage license, " Arthur said in a stern voice.

I didn't know how to answer Arthur. For some reason I never thought of looking for a marriage license. I guess it was because I knew they had been married as slaves. I had made an assumption that such a record did not exist. I learned a hard lesson. In genealogy, never let circumstances trick you into assuming that a document doesn't exist.

"Where did you find that information,?" I asked.

"In the courthouse. I'm sitting here with it right now, " Arthur said.

"Where are you now,?" I asked.

"I'm at 5 North Third Street," he said

I departed the office quickly. In a matter of minutes, I was at 5 North Third Street.

"Frank came back from lunch and stuck his head in the door and told me not to forget to put Freejoe in the calendar. I said what the hell do you know about Freejoe? He said he had just talked to his great, great, great grandson and I told him you were doing a calendar and he said don't forget Freejoe. Of course I've already got Joe in the calendar, " Arthur said. Arthur was slender, a little over six feet in height, and he wore glasses.

"Man....two or three people told me that I should get in touch with you and every time I go to the library, you had just been there. I just happened to mention you to Frank and he told me that you worked in his office, " I said.

"Here is the marriage license, number 904. They got married on April 18, 1835, " Arthur said handing me a copy of the license.

I looked at the license.

"This is unbelievable, " I said looking at the document.

"That's something else! I've found quite a few free blacks but Joe was the first black family that I found, " Arthur said leaning back in his chair.

I left Arthur's office with a copy of the marriage license. Meeting Arthur Webb was a turning point in my search for Freejoe. Arthur was a veteran researcher. It was good to have someone you could compare notes with. Something strange was going on. I was getting assistance in my search from people that I knew and some I had never met. I was convinced I had to write a book. I had to tell the world about Joseph "Freejoe" Harris. Injustice and time had formed a partnership and participated in a conspiracy of silence to cover up the accomplishments of this incredible man. I began to think of Alex Haley. "Roots" wasn't just a novel to me anymore. It was real. I began to think of the anxieties I had felt before mother's death. Now I knew why I was in Memphis. I was here to bring Joseph "Freejoe" Harris out of the dark tunnel of time into a bright new day.

CHAPTER THIRTEEN

MEETING AT MURFREESBORO

" Do not err, my beloved brethren", **James 1:16**

Murfreesboro was a quiet little town not far from Tennessee's state capital. The director's meeting would adjourn at noon and I had no plans for lunch. A good breakfast would tide me over until I reached home. The dining room at the hotel was almost empty. I was almost finished with my breakfast.

"Director Lacey! Good morning, " Phillip said cheerfully. Phillip Johnson was the International Trade director. He was short in stature with a receding hair line. He was a cheerful fellow with a broad smile.

"Good morning, Director Johnson, " I said smiling.

"Do you mind if I join you,?" Phillip inquired pulling out a chair.

"No, no. Have a seat. This place is almost empty, " I said.

"I needed more than coffee and rolls this morning, " Phillip said smiling.

"I know what you mean. I did too. I have no plans to stop for lunch when the meeting is over, " I said continuing to eat.

"How is your book coming,?" Phillip inquired smiling.

"It's coming along fine, thank you, " I replied.

"You know I've heard so much about Alex Haley's book, "Roots". So many people are saying that he made up most of that stuff. How do you feel about that,?" Phillip asked.

"Well ......if you had asked that question about 12 years ago, I might have believed that myself, but based on what I know now, I would say that what people are saying isn't true. His book is authentic," I said authoritatively.

"You know they say his book is based almost entirely on oral history, " Phillip said.

"I know. As a genealogist, whenever you receive oral history, you have the responsibility of checking out the authenticity of the information. However, if you fail in that attempt, you use it anyway because 90 percentage of the time your source is reliable, " I said.

Phillip listened attentively to my explanation.

"For an example, there is a man that lives in Arlington, Tennessee, who is almost 98 years old and has been a member of Gray's Creek Baptist Church all his life. He told me that when the whites had the church, it was known as a Camelot church, " I said.

"What's this man's name,?" Phillip asked.

"His name is Robert Johnson, " I said.

"And he said Camelot church...Are you sure that's what he said,?" Phillip asked sternly.

"That's what it sounded like to me. I've been looking for more than six months for information on that church, " I said.

"Ha, ha, ha. I'd be willing to bet you that he wasn't saying Camelot. He was saying Campbellite, " Phillip said.

"Campbellite! " I said surprised.

"Yes...Campbellite. Campbell was a minister and everyone who followed him was referred to as a Campbellite, " Phillip said.

"What was his first name?," I asked.

"I don't remember. I can find out and give you a call, " Phillip said.

Phillip and I finished our breakfast and I went back up to my room to prepare for our meeting. I came down a few moments later, and took a seat next to the director from Dyersburg State College, Bob Wylie.

"Good morning Bob, " I said.

"Good morning Earnest, " Bob replied. Bob was of medium build with hair that looked like silver. He was very pleasant to talk to and I enjoyed his company.

THE SEARCH FOR FREEJOE

"I trust you and Janie had a good evening, " I said. Janie is Bob's wife and whenever Elaine would accompany me on these trips, the two ladies would spend time together.

"We had a pretty nice evening. We found this little restaurant not far from here. The food was good and the prices were reasonable, " Bob said choosing his words carefully and using a low tone of voice.

"Good, " I said.

"Janie said to tell Elaine hello. She asked me if Elaine came on the trip and I told her you said she had to work, " Bob said.

"She wanted to come, but she had to work, " I said.

"There is something I've been wanting to ask you about. It slipped my mind yesterday. How are you coming on your book?," Bob asked.

"The book is coming along fine. This must be the day to answer questions on the book. Phillip Johnson and I just had a discussion on the book. We were talking about oral history and he was telling me about a man named Campbell, " I said.

"Did you say Campbell?," Bob said.

"Yes. He was a minister during the 1800s. Phillip couldn't remember his first name, " I said.

"Alexander Campbell. I know a little something about him. He was the leader of the restoration movement and he was founder of the Christian Church and the Desciples of Christ Church. He started a school in Bethany, Virginia. I believe it's West Virginia now, " Bob said.

"Thanks. I'm going to do some research on this fellow, " I said.

"You are going to find him very interesting, " Bob said.

The meeting started and thoughts of my conversations with Phillip Johnson and Bob Wylie began to surface in my mind. I departed Murfreesboro for Memphis and the entire trip consisted of thoughts of Alexander Campbell and what role he played in the life of Freejoe Harris. Perhaps I would find the answer in the main library.

"Good morning Jim. You are just the person I want to see, " I said excitedly.

"Good morning Earnest. What can I do for you this morning?," Jim asked cheerfully. Dr. Jim Johnson was manager of the history department at the main library in Memphis. He was of medium build, with thinning brown hair. He looked to be on the sunny side of 50 and he was knowledgeable and helpful.

"I'm looking for information on a man named Alexander Campbell, " I said.

"Alexander Campbell. Oh yes, I believe we do have a biography or two on him, " Jim said.

"I understand that he wrote some newsletters, " I said.

"You are right. He did. However, we don't have any of his newsletters, " Jim said.

"Do you know where I can find them?," I asked.

"I have no idea, " Jim said as I walked to a vacant table.

I began to browse through the books Jim had given me. Suddenly I could feel someone standing over me. I looked up.

"Are you writing a book on Alexander Campbell?," the gentleman asked.

"No, I'm not. I'm writing a book on my great, great, great grandfather. I believe Alexander Campbell influenced his ministry, " I replied.

"Go over to Harding University Graduate School of Religion on Park and Cherry road. They have all his newsletters, " the gentleman said.

I thanked the gentleman for the information and continued to browse through the books Jim had provided. I felt someone standing over me again. When I looked up, I could see the same gentleman had returned.

"History owes Campbell his due, " the gentleman said and walked away.

I just sat and watched speechless as the gentleman walked away. Months had passed since that encounter. After reading all of Alexander Campbell's newsletters, I had to agree with the gentleman. History does owe Alexander Campbell his due. The similarities in the lives of Alexander Campbell and Joseph" Freejoe" Harris are too numerous to ignore or dismiss as a coincidence.

CHAPTER FOURTEEN

GREAT, GREAT, GREAT GRANDSONS

"Do not err, my beloved brethren", **James 1:16**

I decided to make one more trip to Goochland County. Since I knew no one in the Goochland County area, something had to be done to inform the citizens of Goochland County about the research I had been doing on my great, great, great, grandfather, Joseph "Freejoe" Harris.

In a conversation with Sharon Taylor-McKinney, a communications and marketing consultant, she suggested that I contact the print media in Goochland County and Richmond. Sharon notified the media of my planned trip to the area. She was also able to identify all activities related to genealogy that would be going on during my stay in the area.

The day following our arrival in Richmond, my wife and I attended a genealogical seminar at the Virginia Historical Society. We were waiting for the session to start.

"You must be Earnest Lacey, " said a tall well dressed gentleman, extending his hand.

"Yes, I am " I said standing to greet the gentleman and extending my hand.

"This is my wife Elaine, " I said motioning to Elaine.

"I am Dr. Preston Leake. I was told that you all would be here today, " Preston said sitting down next to me. Preston was a distinguished looking fellow. He informed me that he was a chemist consultant.

"I understand you are researching your great, great, great, grandfather and some Leake descendants, " he said.

"That's right. My great, great, great grandmother Fanny was a slave on the Leake plantation in Goochland County. I'm looking for additional information on the two Leakes, Richard and Samuel, that moved to Shelby County, Tennessee," I said beginning to gaze at the bag sitting on the floor.

Preston opened the bag he was carrying. He pulled out his desk top computer.

"Did you say Richard?," Preston asked.

"Yes, ...Richard Leake, " I said.

Preston hit a few keys on his computer.

"I don't have anything on Richard. What was the other brother's name?," Preston asked.

" His name was Samuel. His wife's name was Sarah, " I said.

Preston looked into his computer again as I watched over his shoulder.

"I don't have anything on Samuel either, " Preston said.

"Tell you what. When I get back to Memphis, I'll send you copies of the information I have on Samuel and Richard, " I said.

"I would appreciate that, " Preston said.

We sat through the seminar and afterwards, we were given a tour of the Virginia Historical Society facility. It was very impressive. We were almost finished with the tour.

"Excuse me. Are you Earnest Lacey from Memphis?," inquired a young gentleman.

"Yes, I am, " I replied.

"I'm Gary Robertson from the *Richmond Times-Dispatch* I talked to you at your hotel last night, " Gary said extending his hand.

"We sure did. This is my wife Elaine, " I said extending my hand.

"How do you do ma'am?, " Gary said with a smile.

"Fine. It was nice meeting you. I'll finish up the tour and come back later, " Elaine said walking off.

Gary and I found a nice corner off to ourselves. I began to talk about Freejoe as Gary began to put together the story that appeared in the May 30, 1993 edition of the *Richmond Times-Dispatch*.

Before my wife and I departed for Memphis, Marian Lumpkin, a reporter, did a full length story that appeared in *The Goochland Gazettee* newspaper. My wife and I paid a visit to The Goochland County Historical Society on the Courthouse Green in Goochland. The converted building served as a jail during the time Freejoe resided in Goochland County as a slave.

Not long after the article appeared in the Richmond Times-dispatch I received a telephone call from an elated John David Leake who lived in Mechanicsville, Virginia. He has agreed to show me around the old Leake property on my next trip to Richmond.

Before the year ended in 1993, my efforts were helped considerably by the arrival of Sylvester Lewis, a retired cousin from Detroit. He was another source of oral history and with his ability to sketch what his eyes had seen, he was able to capture the house that Freejoe lived in before he died.

"I remember that house. It was torn down about thirty years ago. It stood just west of Airline road, " Sylvester said gleefully. Sylvester was a little less than six feet in height, with short curly hair mingled with gray and he wore glasses.

"Man that is something and you can remember it. Can you draw a sketch of it?," I asked.

"Sure I can. I'll get started on it right away ",Sylvester said.

"I told Charlie Morris that you remembered the house and he told me that he was born in the house, " I said. Charlie Morris was a FreeJoe descendant that came into the family through the Branch line. Martha Harris, a daughter of Freejoe and Fanny Harris, had married George Branch.

"That's possible because cousins Frankie and Walter Branch lived in that house after Mattie(Martha) died. And Mattie was one of Freejoe's daughters, " Sylvester said.

"That's right. She was next to the baby, " I said. "This research on Freejoe gets stranger by the day."

I had met and talked to Leakes in Virginia, but none in Shelby County.

"The time has come for me to talk to some Leakes right here in Shelby County, " I said.

"How do you think you will find them? You don't have the first name, " Elaine said.

"Samuel Leake was a carpenter and he lived in Collierville. I'm going to look for a relative in that field of work that lives in Collierville, " I said.

I began to look in the telephone book for Collierville. I had just begun, when a name got my attention,"John Leake architect." That's him, I said to myself. I called the number, but got no answer.

"I found my man. There is a fellow listed in Collierville who is an architect. I called and no one answered, " I said.

"You are sure he's the one, " Elaine said.

"He's an architect. Samuel Leake was a carpenter. We tend to be what our ancestors were. Look at Freejoe. He was a carpenter, farmer, businessman and minister. The whole family is loaded with all four, " I said proudly.

Several days passed without being able to reach John Leake.

Then, I decided to try contacting him again.

"Hello, " said a male voice on the other end of the telephone.

"Hello. I'm trying to reach a John Leake, " I said.

"I'm John Leake, " he said.

"Mr. Leake are you by any chance related to a man named Samuel Leake?, " I asked.

"I'm the great, great, great, grandson of Samuel Leake, " John said.

"My name is Earnest Lacey and I am the great, great, great grandson of Joseph "Freejoe" Harris. Have you ever heard of him?," I asked.

"I sure have, " John replied.

"In what way?", I asked.

"His name came up when the research was done on Greenlevel. Before Greenlevel could be placed on the National Register, a complete history had to be done on the house, " John said. Greenlevel was the house that was built around 1840. It's on Collierville/Arlington Road, in Collierville, Tennessee.

John and I agreed to meet. I met him at his house and we sat and chatted for about two hours. We even took pictures together. John gave me the telephone number of an aunt, Lillie Mae Leake-Morris who lives in Madina, Tennessee. Lillie Mae talked to me at length about Sucky. She remembered that Sucky was Freejoe's oldest daughter. Sucky was described to me as a petite woman, with high cheek bones. I was told that her Indian features were obvious. Sucky's real name was Susan Harris. She was born in Goochland County in 1828, married Simpson Moore and died in Shelby County, Tennessee in 1916.

CHAPTER FIFTEEN

GRAY'S CREEK MISSIONARY BAPTIST CHURCH

" Do not err, my beloved brethren", **James 1:16**

It was Sunday now. My wife and I had decided that we would worship at Gray's Creek Baptist Church in Eads. As always visitors were asked to stand and give the name of their church home. Reverend Wylie L. Harris, the pastor at Gray's Creek Baptist Church knew that I was a member of Mississippi Boulevard Christian Church in Memphis.

Reverend Harris has been pastor at Gray's Creek Baptist church for many years. After an inspiring message, the doors of the church were open for new members. That phase of the service was now complete and Reverend Harris stood at the podium glancing at his watch.

"It's not quite one o'clock. We have brother Lacey and his lovely wife visiting with us today. Brother Lacey is writing a book. He's writing a book on Freejoe Harris. Brother Lacey has been tracking Freejoe for a long time. We're going to ask brother Lacey to come forward and speak to us about his progress on the book. This will only take a few minutes as we prepare to close our service. "Come on brother Lacey," said Reverend Harris, a well dressed man of medium build who always greeted you with a smile.

I rose from my seat near the rear of the church and came forward and stood at a podium that had been provided. I welcomed the opportunity to share with others, the book I was writing and in the church where my great, great, great grandfather had pastored over a 120 twenty years before.

"Reverend Harris, members of the pulpit, members and friends, brothers and sisters. It's good to be in the house of the Lord one more time. Earlier during the service I was reading the names on the list of the sick and shut-in in the church bulletin. I can related to many of the names on the list because they are the same surnames I came across in the 1870 census when all people in this country were free. There is so much history in West Tennessee and in

Eads and in this church. I could never write a story about Freejoe without including Gray's Creek Baptist Church and the people of Eads. I believe you will be proud of this book. Over 60 chapters have been written and only God knows how many it will take to complete this book. Pray for me and this effort. Thank you, " I said returning to my seat.

"We are certainly praying for brother Lacey. Brother Lacey told me that when this book is published, Airline Road and Highway 64 will never be the same. This will be a busy spot," Reverend Harris said, smiling.

After a few handshakes and greetings, we were on our way back home. Another writing session was awaiting me.

CHAPTER SIXTEEN

THE UPPER ROOM

"Do not err, my beloved brethren", **James 1:16**

"Lacey speaking, " I said answering the telephone.

"Earnest......Myra Quick, " Myra said cheerfully.

"Hello Myra. What can I do for you?," I asked.

"I know that you are writing a book, so I called to let you know that we have a writer coming to the University to teach a class on how to write a book. He's going to do three different sessions. The sessions are primarily for first time or beginning writers. You can sign up for one, two or all three sessions " Myra said.

Myra was a program developer in the continuing education department for the University of Memphis. She is an intelligent and polite woman in her late thirties or early forties, with short light brown hair. I had met her when I came to the center and over the years we had become good friends.

"Why don't you send me some information on the sessions, " I said.

"Copies of the fall schedule will be available next week. I'll bring a supply by your office. I do hope that you will attend because this guy is really good," Myra said.

"What's his name?," I asked.

"Tom Bird. He lives in Kill Devils Hill, North Carolina, " Myra said.

A few days later, Myra came by the office with a supply of the Continuing Education Fall Schedule. Two of the three sessions peeked my interest. The first session was on a Friday evening. The large lecture hall was filling rapidly. Down front was a young European-American male. His hair was semi-long, falling slightly over his ears. He was milling around, stopping every few seconds as the room continued to fill up with beginning writers. I had expected the presenter to be much older.

It was six o'clock. Time to begin the Friday session. Tom Bird had been introduced. The young presenter began to speak.

"I went to college to become a writer. After four years and a degree, I still couldn't write. After I graduated from college, I went to work in public relations for the Pittsburgh Pirates. I worked for them for three years and they paid me well, but in the back of my mind, I wanted to be a writer. One day I prayed to God and ask him to show me how to write and I would show others. I have been writing ever since that day. There was a time that I seriously thought about not teaching anymore, but I love doing this as well as I do writing, "Tom said.

Tom was very impressive. He was witty. He kept his students interest running high throughout the session. I was impressed with him because he had done something that professionals seldom do, give a testimony in public to God. It was time for a break. At break time, it was time to converge on the teacher with private comments or questions.

"Mr. Bird",....I'm Earnest Lacey, " I said extending my hand as Myra stood nearby smiling.

"Pleased to meet you Earnest, " Tom said extending his hand with a smile.

"You said you prayed to God and asked him to help you become a writer and in exchange you promised God that you would help others become writers. You also said that at one time you were thinking of giving up teaching, but you had grown to love it, " I said.

"That's right, " Tom said smiling.

"I'm glad you didn't stop teaching, " I said.

"I'm glad I didn't either, " Tom said with a slight laugh.

"Because if you had, your success as a writer would have turned to failure. I'm not a preacher and I don't consider myself a student of the Bible, but when you prayed to God and asked him to help you, you entered into an agreement with God. You asked God for something and he gave it to you in exchange for you to do something for him. You negotiated with God. Had you broken your promise to him, God could have and he would have broken his promise to you. Many times we think we are praying, when all we are doing is begging, because we offer nothing to God in exchange for what we want. Dealing with God is serious business, " I said.

"I never thought of it that way. I find that very interesting, " Tom said.

I returned the following morning for the second and last session. I've been in touch with Tom several times since the classes. Tom impressed upon me, that I and only I could write " Freejoe". No one else could do what God had called me to do.

After my sessions with Tom Bird , I began to write in earnest. I felt good. I felt like I had a mission to fulfill. I began to use the techniques I had been taught in class. I went to the quietest place in my house. The upper room .....where the radio and television was turned off. The upper room......where telephone calls and interruptions weren't allowed. The upper room.....where prayer and meditation was a prerequisite before I picked up my pen. The upper room.....where God and the spirits of my ancestors convened and formulated the ideas that I transposed into the written word. The upper room..... where I heard the cries of my people for deliverance. The upper room.... where I heard those that toiled in the field whisper to one another, " Lincoln is the deliverer". The upper room....where tears flowed like water down a mighty stream. The upper room .....where emotions ran high and I paced the floor until they were no more. The upper room......where the opening of the door meant that another page on another chapter had been completed on a man and his times, Joseph "Freejoe" Harris, 1796-1875.

PART II
Geneology

GENEOLOGY

G enealogy is an account or record which traces the ancestry of a certain individual or family; descent from an ancestor; lineage ; pedigree; the study of pedigrees or family history.

Genealogy not only defines who we are, it tells us who we have been. The very essence of our existence is linked to our past, our ancestors. We are now who they used to be. Many of our characteristics, talents, physical elements and vocations can be directly attributed to our ancestors. The past, present and future will always have a role in our lives. These segments of time are bound together and for our family, it is all one.

When we trace our family line down through time, we establish and strengthen the bonds of kinship, as well as elevate our own personal self-esteem. A major appeal of genealogy is that it provides people with a sense of pride, continuity and of belonging. You don't really grow up to be somebody, you are somebody....... based on your own family lineage.

Popular interest in genealogy was stimulated during the 1970's by the television dramatization of Alex Haley's, "Roots". Haley traced his ancestry back to his African ancestors. Interest in genealogy is not new. In the first book of the Old Testament, Genesis is an account of lineage running from Adam to Abraham. In the New Testament, Matthew devotes the first 16 verses of Chapter One to tracing the ancestors of Jesus from King David through 42 generations. There are 14 generations from Abraham to David; 14 generations from David to the Babylonian exile, and 14 generations from the Babylonian exile until the Christ.

Primitive societies recognized the importance of genealogy by organizing themselves into tribes and clans. They often sought to trace their ancestry to gods, legendary heroes or animals.

Lineage was originally transmitted by oral tradition, but later literate societies began to write them down. Notable early western examples include the genealogies of the tribes of Israel (recorded in the Bible), the Greeks and the Romans. Genealogies assumed particular importance in connection with the principle of inheritance—of power, rank and property.

In modern times, social status has depended less on pedigree, but genealogy remains of interest to many people other than scholars. The United States, for an example, has a number of genealogical societies which traces people's descent. Many patriotic organizations, such as the Daughters of the American Revolution, limit membership to descendants of a particular historical group. The Mormon church has collected an enormous bank of genealogical data such as registers of births, marriages, deaths, and other related documents. This collection is the largest collection in existence. Many local libraries also have many large collections.

While the hardships of slavery happened more than a century ago, the obstacles continue to be felt as generations today try to piece together their family history.

I have also faced the task of slowly piecing together my family history, after learning about my ancestry in 1984, through family members who knew very little about our beginning. Such research has led me to information about my great-great-great-grandfather, which reveals his many accomplishments during the era of slavery and beyond.

Slavery can not and must not be used as a barrier in your quest to reach your goal. Researching your family requires you to make a commitment to finish the task that you begin. Now that you know why genealogy is important and the role it plays in our family life, let me help you research your family.

LACEY'S 15 STEPS ALONG THE ANCESTRAL TRAIL

"How to gather your family history"

1.) Your search begins with you. What you already know. Start with yourself and work backwards. Secure a family group sheet from the library or local genealogical society. Get your parents, grandparents, and great grandparents to talk about their parents, siblings and early beginnings.

2.) Get a good tape recorder for gathering oral histories. Plan all interviews. Prepare a list of questions to ask. Turn the recorder on at family gatherings such as reunions, Thanksgiving, Christmas, etc.

3.) Census Records are perhaps the most widely used genealogical records. The national archives is the custodian of millions of records of people that have had dealings with the Federal Government. Many of these records are housed in the National Archives in Washington, DC. and the 11 regional offices around the country. These records may also be found in your local library. Indian, land, naturalization, passenger lists, personnel records and Armed Services records are also housed by the Federal Government. Currently the U.S. census from 1790 to 1920 is available. The only exception is the census of 1890. Those records were destroyed by fire. The 1870 census is the first census to list all persons in this country. Free persons of color can be found in the census prior to 1870. This is an excellent resource, but like many records, there are errors that you can expect. Many names are misspelled and ages of family members can be incorrect. Many of the census takers were uneducated and gathered information from third parties, even children. Nicknames were substituted for real or given names. Names given to our ancestors had special meanings. There are books available on the origin and meaning of names, both surnames and given names.

4.) Record maiden names. Many females are lost in history because they only carry their married names. Birth certificates and death certificates can yield these, but beware, there is a possibility of error. This is secondary information.

5.)   Check Death Records. They can assist in compiling a family medical history, including identification of current family illnesses. Death and birth certificates did not become a required document until earlier in this century, but some states required them much earlier. The death certificate is only as good as the informant supplying the information. In our search to find a loved one, if we know the location he or she died in, we can search through the obituaries of old newspapers, and contact the local funeral home or homes. If the person died in recent years and you knew his or her occupation, they may have been a member of a particular labor union. Seek out the labor union for assistance. Always keep in mind that the death certificate will be filed where the death occurred. A person can live in one location all their life and die on a visit or vacation.

6.)   Visit the Cemetery. Record all similar surnames and the names of persons buried within 20 feet of your loved one. Many relatives not only lived close by, but many died and were buried close by one another. We may not recognize many of these names in our early research, but those names could show up on a birth certificate, death certificate or in probate records later in your research.

7.)   Look at School Records. They are becoming available for inspection. This is an excellent source of primary data.

8.)   Social Security Administration records are available on deceased persons and these records can be cross-referenced with other records. A copy of the application of the deceased can be obtained. These are excellent primary records.

9.)   SLAVE PERIOD: Check slave schedules by state, county and surname. Check probate records of your ancestor's plantation owner or owners and their children. Check plantation owner or owners' tax records on property. Slaves were considered property. Slave schedules were made available during the 1850 and 1860 census. In addition to comparing them to probate inventories, they could be used for comparative purposes for tax rolls, since there was a tax levied against slaves because they were considered property, bills of sales and in order to identify owners with the same given names and surnames. I consider the Probate Records the best tool to use during the slave period to find an ancestor. Many loved ones are in the inventory among the assets of the deceased plantation owner. Many slaves are listed by name, value and description. The relationship between slaves are sometimes given.

10.) Marriage Records. The information we receive or gather from a marriage document will depend to a great extent on the amount of information required on the application by individual states. Many times we find marriage information published in the newspapers. It's interesting to note who performed the wedding ceremony. If the wedding takes place at a church, there could be additional family information on the church register. This information could lead us to the church of a loved one. It could also lead us to a gold mine of information on the family which could be contained among church records of all sorts. In our search for marriage records it is good to know the various requirements in a county or state at a particular time. For an example, some counties within a state require that a bond be posted. Not everyone could afford to post a bond, so they went to a county within the state where requirements were less of a financial strain. Some may have went to a neighboring state. Check the archives for books on consummated marriages for a particular time period. Marriages of free people of African descent that took place before the Emancipation Proclamation can be found in these records. Many people of African descent who were classified as slaves prior to the Emancipation Proclamation, had their marriages legitimized through the Freemen's Bureau. This occurred from 1865-1875. A special note to Caucasians. Don't overlook the Freemen's Bureau records. Many Caucasians in slave holding states used the Bureau.

11.) Military Records are another source of genealogical information. Many states have records housed in their archives that pertain to veterans of their states. Records are available for:

The Revolutionary War
The War of 1812
Mexican War
Cherokee Removal Muster Rolls
State Militia
Civil War
World War I

There are many records available on those that served in the Civil War, both Caucasian Europeans and African Americans for the Union and the Confederacy. The pension records contain the family history of those who fought these battles.

12.) Agricultural Schedules will assist you in the documentation of land holdings, property tax rolls, probate inventories and distinguish between people of similar names. These schedules tell us what was grown, what was raised, how much and its value. These schedules are available for the census years of 1850, 1860, 1870 and 1880 by state.

13.) Manufacturing Schedules are sometimes referred to as industry schedules. These schedules will tell us the location of the business, type of equipment, number of employees, what was manufactured and the annual production. These schedules are also available for the census years of 1850, 1860, 1870 and 1880 by state.

14.) Social Statistics Schedules cover 1.) Cemeteries; where they are within a city, when they closed and why? 2.) Trade societies and clubs. Also lodges with names of members and officers and 3.) Churches, how and when they were founded. These schedules are available for the census years of 1850, 1860, 1870 and 1880 by state.

15.) Make copies of the data you've found. You lessen the chance of making errors. Network with other researchers because it plays a big role in your ancestral search.

LEGAL TERMS USED IN GENEALOGY RESEARCH

Abstract = A summary of the important points in a will, deed, or other documents.

Administration = The management and disposal, under legal authority, of a deceased person's estate.

Administrator = A person to whom letters of administration (authority to administer a deceased person's estate) have been granted by the proper court.

Bill of Sale = A written agreement whereby one transfers his right to or interest in personal goods or chattels to another.

Bond = A document with a sum of money affixed as a penalty binding the parties to pay that sum if certain acts are not performed.

Deed = Document whereby title in real property (land) is transferred from one party to another. Also called a conveyance and an Indenture.

Dower = A life estate which a widow has in one- third of all the lands of her late husband for the support of herself and her children.

Estate = The Sum total or aggregate of a person's property.

Executor = A person named by the testator in his will to see that the provisions of the will are carried out after his death. A woman who is named by the testator to carry out this function is known as the Executrix.

Fee Simple = An estate in land which has the potential of lasting forever. The owner is entitled to the property to do with it as he wishes.

Goods and Chattels = The most comprehensive description of personal property.

Guardian = A person charged with responsibility for managing the rights and property of a minor or a person incapable of handling his own affairs.

Heir = A person who succeeds to or inherits the possession of property, through legal means, after another's death.

Intestate = A person who dies without making a will.

Orphan = A minor or infant who has lost one or both of his parents.

Petition = A formal written request or supplication made by an inferior to a superior and especially to one having jurisdiction.

Probate = Originally, to prove before the proper court that a "Last will and testament" of a deceased person was indeed what it purported to be. In American law, it is used as an inclusive term to describe all matters over which a probate court has jurisdiction.

Quitclaim Deed = An instrument by which a person releases all title, interest or claim which he may possess in certain real properties.

Realty = Relating to land. The most comprehensive term for real estate appearing in old deeds is lands, tenements, and hereditaments.

Release = A document by which a person gives up, to another, his right to something in which he has a just claim.

Relict = A widow; Sometimes used, but rarely, to describe a widower.

Surety (or Security) = a person who makes himself liable for another person's debts or obligations should the first default.

Testate = To die leaving a valid will is to die testate.

Testament = A will, or disposition, of personal property. It is used generally as equivalent to "will."

Trust Deed = A type of mortgage. They operate by placing the title to real property in one or more trustees to secure the payment of a debt.

Ward = An infant who is under guardianship.

Will = A declaration of a person's wishes concerning the disposition of his property after death. Originally it related to the disposition of real estate. The popular designation, whether or not it relates to both real and personal property, is "last will and testament."

RESEARCH CHECKLIST

Location of sources:

Home

County records

Town records and Libraries

Church depositories

Type of source:

Family bible
Family letters
Interviews
Photographs

Vital records
Marriage records
Wills, estates, etc.
Deeds, etc.
Mortgages
Other recorders' records
Naturalization records

City or county directories
Cemetery records/grave.
  Insc.
Miscellaneous Or published
  histories
Newspaper files
Tax lists
Voter records
Public school records

Archives
Local parish records
Local church histories

State records

Vital records
Land grants
State census
Militia records
Tax lists
Archives
Acts, journals

National records

Censuses
Mortality schedules
Military records
Pension records
Passenger lists
Immigration records
Land records
Special records

Libraries

Indexes, special
Printed & miscellaneous
   Genealogies
Printed histories
Occupational histories
Biographical compendia
Manuscript histories
Obituary collections/graves.
   insc.

Abstract volumes

THE SOUNDEX SYSTEM

The soundex system is a filing system that keeps together names of the same and similar sounds but of variant spellings. The first letter of the surname is alphabetic and numeric afterwards. The first letter of a surname is not coded. Every soundex number is a 3-digit number.

Soundex Coding Guide

Code	Key letters and Equivalents
1	b, p, f, v
2	c, s, k, g, j, q, x, z
3	d, t
4	l
5	m, n
6	r

The letters a, e, i, o, u, y, w, and h are not coded.

THE U.S. FEDERAL CENSUS:

The U.S. Federal Census is the most frequently used Federal record. The census is taken because it was mandated by the United States Constitution. President George Washington signed the act into law in 1790. One of the main goals of the census was to provide information on men eligible for the military. The census is taken every 10 years, in the year ending with zero. Some individual states took their own census in the years between the federal enumeration. Much of the 1790 Census was destroyed by the British during the War of 1812. The census of 1890 was also destroyed. You might consider using tax lists as an alternate source for those periods. Census records must remain private for 72 years. This is done to encourage accurate and truthful information.

THE SEARCH FOR FREEJOE

The 1790-1840 census lists the name of the head of household. In the 1850 census all persons in each household are listed by name. The birthplace for each person is also listed. The 1870 census asks about the birthplace of parents. In the 1880 census everyone lists their relationship to the Head of the Household, their marital status, their actual place of birth and the place of birth for parent. The census of 1890 was destroyed by fire. In the 1900 census, each family was assigned an identification number and each census sheet lists the county as well as town or township. This census asks many new questions such as the number of years married, mother of how many children, number of children living, year of immigration, number of years in the U.S., number of months employed, attended school (months), can read, can write, can speak English, home owned or rent? home owned free or mortgage? and farm or house? In the 1910 census, living Civil war veterans are identified as well as the blind and deaf-mute. The 1920 census lists employer, salary worker, or working on own account. To date, there are 12 federal census available for us to review.

Virginia is a key state for researchers with African American roots. In 1790, at the time of the first census, 40 percent of all African Americans in the United States lived in Virginia. Most of them were slaves. African Americans, both enslaved and free, have lived in Virginia from the earliest times. The first African immigrants to the United States arrived in 1619 at Jamestown in a Dutch Frigate. Some 75 percent of African Americans have at least one white ancestor and 15 percent have a predominately white ancestry. In addition, more than 60 percent of African Americans have a mixture of Indian blood in their veins.

We really are more than who we think we are. Take another look at the person in the mirror. You are more than the eye can see. You are all the ancestors that came before you and you will be a part of all of those that come after you. You are not the beginning and you are not the end. Just somewhere in between.

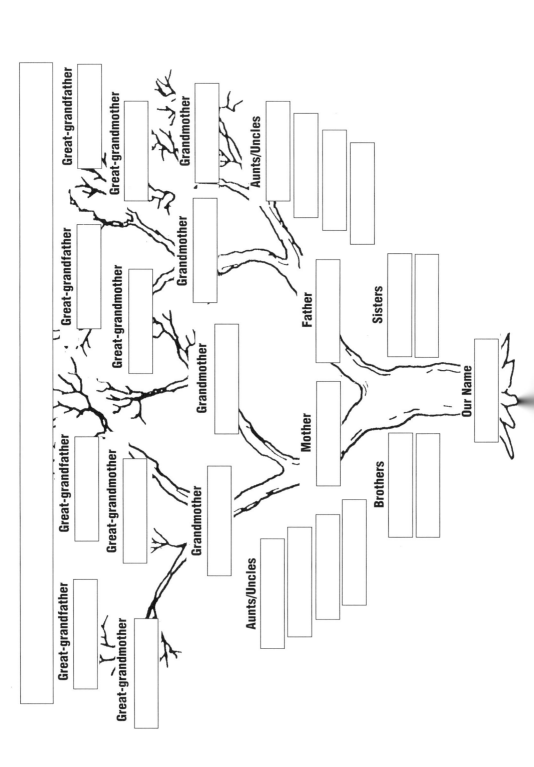

FAMILY GROUP SHEET

HUSBAND'S NAME _____   WIFE'S MAIDEN NAME _____
Date of Birth _____   Date of Birth _____
Place _____   Place _____
Date of Birth _____   Date of Birth _____
Place _____   Place _____
Present Address _____   Present Address _____
Place of Burial _____   Place of Burial _____
His Father _____   Her Father _____
His Mother's Maiden name _____   Her Mother's Maiden Name _____

Date of Marriage _____

Place _____

Another Marriage   by Husband ☐   By Wife ☐

Did the Couple Divorce?   Yes ☐   No ☐   When? _____

Items of Interest (List Below): _____

_____

_____

Additional Information:

Children (arrange in order of birth)	Birth Information (Give place and when)	Death Information	Marriage Information (Give name of spouse and place)

PART III
Photos and Documents

Peter Harris was born into slavery in June of 1823 in Goochland County, Virginia. He was the oldest child and son of Joseph "Freejoe" and Fanny Harris. He married Louisa Jones in 1843. This union produced 9 children of which 8 can be accounted for. Peter died on January 15, 1902 in Shelby County, Tennessee. He was buried in Zion Cemetery in Memphis, Tennessee.

Louisa Jones-Harris was born into slavery in Virginia in 1829. She and Peter were married for 59 years. Louisa died on July 28, 1912 in Shelby County, Tennessee. Place of burial is unknown.

Virgina Harris-Phillips, the daughter of Joseph "FreeJoe" and Fanny Harris, was born on a wagon train bound for Shelby County, Tennessee. When Virginia was just a girl and men were educationg their sons, her father Joseph "FreeJoe" Harris took her to Hanover, Indiana and enrolled her into an all girls-school. While in Indiana, Virginia met and married Wesley Phillips on November 15th, 1849. This union produced twelve children. Six boys and six girls. Virginia died on June 2, 1878 and was buried in the Hill Cemetery in Oshtemo Township, Kalamazoo County, Kalamazoo, Michigan.

Wesley H. Phillips, husband of Virginia Harris-Phillips, son-in-law of Joseph "FreeJoe" and Fanny Harris, was born in Georgia. His parents moved the family to Jennings County, Indiana when he was just a boy. Not much is known about Wesley's father. His mother's name was Nancy Phillips and he had an older brother named Henry Phillips. Henry was married to a woman named Rosey and they had two daughters, Elora and Cynthia. On September 2, 1862, during the Civil War, Wesley moved his family to Kalamazoo, Michigan. Wesley died on September 25, 1894 and was buried in the Hill Cemetery in Oshtemo Township, Kalamazoo County, Kalamazoo, Michigan.

Considered the oldest standing brick structure in West Tennessee, this house was built in the 1830's by Joseph "FreeJoe" Harris. This modest two room floor plan is a folk configutation known as Hall and Parlor and included a loft. This design was uncommon in West Tennessee, having appeared during the 1740's in the Tidewater region of Maryland and Virginia. The large hall was used for both mealtimes and informal daily activities, while the smaller parlor had nicer furniture and may also have served as a bedchamber.

Earnest Edward Lacey

Construction techniques of interest included the house's hand made bricks, "sleepers" or log floor joists, and log poles used in the fashioning of roof rafters. The plaster on the walls had been made with horse hair or pig bristles. These elements, crude in execution, exist alongside such careful finishing details as dual-room chair railings and "a penciling technique used in outlining mortar joints on exterior surfaces. The last known private owner of this property was Mary F. Swift, an African-American and a member of the Gray family. She was a descendant of Joseph "FreeJoe" and Fanny Harris.

82

Colonial Samuel Leake was the son of Elisha and Fanny Curd- Leake, grandson of Walter and Judith Mask-Leake, husband of Sarah Johnson-Leake, brother of Richard Leake, father of Catherine Frances (Bagby), Sarah (Moseley), Martha (Moseley), Elisha, Lucy Jane, Virginia, Edward and Tennessee State Senator, Dr. Virginius L. Leake.

Samuel came to Shelby County, Tennessee from Goochland County, Virginia in the early 1830's on a wagon train with his family, his slaves and a freed slave and his family, Joseph "FreeJoe" Harris.

Fanny Harris, the wife of Joseph "FreeJoe" Harris, and their children Peter, James, Susan (Sucky), Adeline (Lettie), and Virginia were slaves on Samuel Leake's plantation. It is believed that Fanny Harris was also a daughter of Samuel Leake. Samuel died in December of 1855 and was buried at a local cemetery. After the death of his wife Sarah, his body was moved and placed beside his wife Sarah in Elmwood Cemetery in Memphis, Tennessee

Sarah Johnson-Leake was the wife of Samuel Leake. She was the mother of Catherine Frances (Bagby), Sarah (Moseley), Martha (Moseley), Lucy Jane, Virginia, Edward and Tennessee State Senator Dr. Virginius L. Leake.

Sarah died on December 18, 1873. She was buried in Elmwood Cemetery in Memphis, Tennessee.

Martha A. Feild-Leake, the wife of Dr. Virginius L. Leake, was a descendant of James Feild, who came to America in 1624 and had two sons, James Feild and Major Peter Feild.

Peter's daughter, Mary married a Jefferson. Her grandson was Peter Jefferson, who married Jane Randolph. Peter Jefferson once served as Sheriff of Goochland County, Virginia. This union produced Thomas Jefferson, 3rd President of the United States of America.

Dr. Virginius L. Leake, the son of Colonial Samue and Sarah Leake, came to Shelby County, Tennessee as a young lad of eleven years of age from Goochland County, Virginia. He became a medical doctor. On October 2,1849, he married Martha A. Feild. On May 1, 1850 Dr. Leake purchased the historic house, "Greenlevel", from his brother-in-law, Bennett Bagby and sister, the former Frances Catherine Leake-Lewis.

After the emancipation, Dr. Leake built a school teach the newly freed slaves how to read, write a do arithmetic.

One of the most notable contributions Dr. Leake made to his community was the donation of lan that is now the town square of Collierville, Tennessee, the fastest growing city in the state.

With the assistance of Joseph "FreeJoe" Harris a the overwhelming vote of the newly freed slaves Dr. Leake was elected to the Tennessee State Senate. This election in 1872 made Dr. Leake th first white politician in the state and among the first in the South, to represent such a large constituency of people of color. Dr. Virginius suffer a massive heart attack in Nashville and was bur in Magnolia Cemetery in Collierville, Tennessee

Millard Feild Leake was born on August 10, 1852 in Shelby County, Tennessee. He was the son of Dr. Virginius L. and Martha Feild-Leake, grandson of Samuel and Sarah Johnson-Leake, husband of Alabama Irby-Leake and father of six children, one girl and five boys.

Millard was a graduate of Virginia Military Institute. He was also an educator, Methodist Minister and surveyor. He surveyed all the lands in the estate of Joseph "FreeJoe" Harris in 1875-1878. Millard died on March 21, 1931 at the age of 78 years. He is buried in Magnolia Cemetery, in Collierville, Tennessee.

"Greenlevel" is an imposing two story Greek Revival house, constructed circa 1830 and embellished with a two story pediment portico around 1850. After Dr. Virginius Leake purchased the house, on May 1, 1850, from Bennett Bagby, His brother-in-law and sister France C. Leake-Lewis, he hired Joseph "FreeJoe" Harris to make several interior and exterior improvements to the house. During the Civil War, "GreenLevel" served as a hospital for Confederate soldiers. After the battle of Shiloh, approximately 119 wounded soldiers were brought from Corinth, Mississippi to "GreenLevel" for treatment. The central hall upstairs was used for surgery and blood stains remain in the floor of the hall today. On March 6, 1987, this house on Collierville-Arlington road in Collierville, Tennessee was placed on the national register of historic places.

Cornelius H. Harris, the son of Joseph "FreeJoe" and Fanny Harris and Emma Minerva Jones-Harris were more than husband and wife. They were also uncle and niece. Cornelius married his sister Lettie's daughter. The marriage took place on December 2, 1865 in Fayette County, Tennessee. This union produced no children. Joseph "FreeJoe" Harris named his son Cornelius executor of his estate. After the death of Cornelius, Emma moved to Grand Rapids, Michigan to live with her sister, Phoebe Anna Jones-Johnson. Cornelius died on February 16, 1907 and Emma died on July 8, 1929. Both are buried in the Cemetery at West Oshtemo Baptist Church in Kalamazoo, Michigan.

Phoebe Anna Jones-Johnson-Taylor was the sister of Emma Minerva Jones-Harris. She was also the sister of Caledonia Frances "Callie" Jones-Lewis, Jefferson M. Jones Jr., Meddicas Jones and James Jones and the niece of Cornelius H. Harris. Phoebe moved to Oshtemo Township, Kalamazoo County, Kalamazoo, Michigan to live with her sister Emma Minerva Jones-Harris and uncle/brother-in-law, Cornelius H. Harris in the early 1870's.

On November 25th, 1891, Phoebe Anna married James N. Johnson, a mulatto from Canada and moved to Grand Rapids, Michigan. During a very serious illness, James deserted Phoebe Anna and returned to Canada. Phoebe recovered and divorced James. She later married a man named Taylor. His first name is unavailable. That marriage ended in divorce.

Phoebe Anna died in 1956 and is buried in the cemetery at West Oshtemo Baptist Church in Kalamazoo, Michigan.

Fannie Phillips, the daughter of Wesley and Virginia Harris-Phillips, was born August 3, 1864. She was a housewife and the mother of two sons and one daughter. Fannie married Albert White He was a building contractor. The date of her death is unknown. Place of burial is unknown.

Ida Phillips, the daughter of Wesley and Virginia Harris-Phillips, was born October 20, 1868. She was a homemaker. Ida married John Moore, a brick mason. She died on June 11, 1912. Place of burial is unknown.

Laura Ellen Phillips, the daughter of Wesley an
Virginia Harris-Phillips, was born September 1♦
1871. She was a homemaker. Laura married
Andrew William Frazier. She died in 1947. Pla
of burial is unknown.

Martha M. Phillips, the daughter of Wesley an♦
Virginia Harris-Phillips, was born January 15,
1857. She was a dress maker with interest in R
Estate. She married William Franklin McDona
That union produced one child, Dolly Abigail
McDonald. Martha died on June 15, 1951. Sh♦
buried in the Hill Cemetery, in Oshtemo
Township, Kalamazoo, Michigan.

Carrie Phillips, the daughter of Wesley and Virginia Harris-Phillips, was born June 14, 1873. She was a homemaker and married Mr. Mills, a construction worker. They moved to New York City, New York. Carrie died in Suffolk, New York. The date is unknown. Place of burial is unknown.

(NOT PICTURE)

Susan Phillips, the daughter of Wesley and Virginia Harris-Phillips, was born August 17, 1875. She was a homemaker. She married William Lewis, a clerk at the Michigan State Capital in Lansing, Michigan. She was the mother of one son and five daughters. Date of death and place of buried is unknown.

Gilmore L. Phillips, son of Wesley and Virginia Harris-Phillips, was born August 10, 1862. He worked in banks all his life. He played the violin and was the manager of the Phillips Brothers Orchestra. He was married to the former Dean Proctor. He died in 1937. Place of burial is unknown.

Joshua W. Phillips, son of Wesley and Virginia Harris-Phillips, was born April 28, 1853. He was a barber at the Michigan State Hospital until he retired. He played the violin. He was married to the former Martha C. Wilson. He died on May 3, 1937. Place of burial is unknown.

Sylvester Clayton Phillips, son of Wesley and Virginia Harris-Phillips, was born April 17, 1855. He was a carpenter. He played bass violin. He was also a singer. Favorite song was "Sleeper In the Down." He was married to the former Elnora Stewart. He died on September 7, 1920. Place of burial is unknown.

Joseph F. Phillips, son of Wesley and Virginia Harris-Phillips, was born on January 5, 1851. He was a cement block contractor. In later years, he was a caretaker for the Stock Bridge home. He played the violin and conducted the church choir for many years. He was married to the former Mary E. Burton. He died on March 21, 1921. Place of burial is unknown.

(NOT PICTURED)

Albert Phillips, son of Wesley and Virginia Harris-Phillips, was born October 17, 1866. He spent most of his life in Indiana and Kentucky as a trainer of race horses. He played the violin and was married to the former Sarah Scott. He died on December 3, 1923. Place of burial is unknown.

Baby Boy Phillips was born May 23, 1878. Died May 26, 1878. He was unnamed. Virginia Harris-Phillips, his mother, died a week later.

William M. Harris was born in slavery on November 15, 1849 on the Samuel Leake plantation, in Shelby County, Tennessee. He was the oldest son of Peter and Louisa Ann Jones-Harris, grandson of Joseph "FreeJoe" and Fanny Harris, brother of Alice (Louis Gray), Sarah (Oscar Branch), John (Laura), Luella (Henry Anderson), Joe (Mary), Virginia and Cornelius (Cassiana) Harris.

Will Anderson (Josie Hayes), Mary Frances (Tucker), Annie (Tatum), Mariah (Jones), Darah (Biggs), Sallie (Branch), Robert L., Benjamin, Zedekiah (Melinda), Joseph (Mattie Pearl Cunningham), Pinkie (Joseph Price), Susie and Verdora Harris were among the approximate 18 children of William Harris.

William was a farmer and traveling preacher. He was also one of the founders of the all Negro town, Mound Bayou, Mississippi. William was married four times. At the time of his death on December 25, 1918, he was married to Nannie Branch-Harris. He is buried in Mt. Pisgah Cemetery at Mt. Pisgah Missionary Baptist church in Cordova, Tennessee.

Anna Russell-Phillips, the daughter-in-law of Wesley and Virginia Harris-Phillips, was the last wife of Sylvester Phillips. She was born in Indiana in September of 1864. Her father was born in North Carolina and her mother in South Carolina. She and Sylvester were married 19 years.

Mary E. Burton-Phillips, Daughter-in-law of Wesley and Virginia Harris-Phillips, was the wife of Joseph Phillips and she was born in February of 1855 in Ohio. The birthplace of her parents is unknown. She and Joseph were married for 44 years.

Dean Proctor-Phillips, Daughter-in-law of Wesley and Virginia Harris-Phillips, was the wife of Gilmore Phillips. They were married 43 years. Dean died on November 19, 1930 from an operation for appendicitis at the New Borgess Hospital in Kalamazoo, Michigan.

Dolly Abigail McDonald, granddaughter of Wesley and Virginia Harris-Phillips and Mother Martha Phillips-McDonald. Martha McDonald was married to William McDonald. Dolly Abigail is 3 months old and the year was 1899.

William Franklin McDonald a resident of Kalamazoo, Michigan was born on June 14, 1863, the son of Franklin and Abigail McDonald, the husband of Martha Marie "Mattie" Phillips-McDonald, son-in-law of Wesley and Virginia Harris-Phillips, grand son-in-law of Joseph "FreeJoe" and Fanny Harris and father of Dolly Abigail McDonald-Brown-Davis.

William was a carpenter and builder, a coachman for the Standard Oil Company, a member of the Allen Chapel AME church for more than 50 years and husband of Martha Marie "Mattie" Phillips-McDonald for 62 years.

William died in 1947 and is buried in the Hill Cemetery in Oshtemo Township, Kalamazoo County, Kalamazoo, Michigan.

Dolly was born on September 3, 1899 in Kalamazoo, Michigan. She was married twice and was preceded in death by Richard Brown and Neil Davis, Sr.

She was the mother of two daughters, Mary Brown-Perkins and Martha Brown-Holt. She had one son, Richard Brown.

She was a member of Allen Chapel AME church for 81 years. At the time of her death, she was Kalamazoo's oldest living African-American citizen.

On October 11, 1997, Dolly passed into eternity and was laid to rest in the Hill cemetery in Kalamazoo, Michigan.

Martha Harris-Branch was born in Eads, Tennessee. She was the daughter of Joseph "FreeJoe" and Fanny Harris, wife of George Branch and mother of Walter, Joe, Fannie, Ada, Mamie, Essie and George Branch.

Martha taught her guitar playing husband George how to read. George later became a Baptist preacher.

After Joseph "FreeJoe" Harris died in 1875, Martha and her husband George moved into his house and continued to run the stagecoach line and the Inn at Airline road and highway 64.

Gray's Creek Cemetery is located north of Gray's Creek Missionary Baptist Church on Airline Road, near the corner of highway 64.

This cemetery was established in February of 1843 and is the oldest African-American cemetery in Shelby County, Tennessee.

One of Shelby County's most prominent citizens during the 1800's, Joseph H. "FreeJoe" Harris is buried here.

This is the final resting place of Wesley H. and Virginia Harris-Phillips, William and Martha Phillips-McDonald, Dolly Abigail McDonald-Brown-Davis and other family members. This cemetery is located in Oshtemo Township, Kalamazoo County, Kalamazoo, Michigan.

Located on highway 64 and Bekemeyer Road, this property was once owned by Joseph "FreeJoe" Harris. According to the fourth paragraph of his will, this property was to be sold to pay off his last remaining debts. A controversy surrounded the selling of this land to two of his children, Peter Harris and Rhoda Green and two of his grand children, Frank Leake and Joseph Lewis. A few years later, Joseph Lewis and his wife "Callie" Frances, purchased the shares of land owned by Peter Harris, Rhoda Green and Frank Leake. This land remained in the Lewis family until the 1960s. At that time due to the efforts of Ethyle Belle Horton-Venson, a grand daughter of Joseph and "Callie" Lewis and a civic leader in Memphis, Tennessee, part of the land was sold and another part donated. Earnest Edward Lacey is a great grandson of Joseph and "Callie" Lewis.

Lucy Ann Claxton, holding a copy of "FreeJoe", a book written on the life of Joseph "FreeJoe" Harris, and a copy of *GRACE* magazine which contains an article on geneology written by Mr. Lacey is the daughter of Dr. Walter P. and Elizabeth Shaw-Claxton; Granddaughter of John W. and Elizabeth Higgason-Shaw and sister of Polly Claxton. Lucy is a resident of Somerville in Fayette County, Tennessee. Born in the early 1900s, Lucy's grandparents knew Joseph "FreeJoe" Harris. "My grandparents often talked about the things he did for them during the Civil War. As a result my late sister Polly and I were required to blow a kiss to that old brick house in the curve on highway 64 every time we went to Memphis. They moved that house to Germantown", Lucy said.

Standing secluded and hidden by undergrowth, oaks and cedars near the Canadaville community, just off Seward Road in the western edge of Fayette County is all that remains of this fascinating house built by Joseph "FreeJoe" Harris prior to 1847. It is empty and open to the elements and has become victimized by vandals and graffiti. It's the oldest known three-story brick structure standing in Fayette County and perhaps in all of West Tennessee.

Earnest Edward Lacey (left) and Rev. Wylie L. Harris (right), pastor of Gray's Creek Missionary Baptist church. Rev. Harris, no relation to Joseph "FreeJoe" Harris, has pastored Gray's Creek Missionary Baptist Church since July of 1977.

Robert E. Johnson II was born on March 15, 1896 in Eads, Tennessee. He was the 11th of 14 children born to Andrew W. and Rosetta Johnson. He was married to Roxie Steward and Pearlester Jones. Neither marriage produced children but he did provide parental love and guidance to three foster children. Mr. Johnson served in the First World War and in 1995 received The World War I Meritorious Service award. He was a member of Gray's Creek Missionary Baptist church, serving as Secretary of the Sunday School, Assistant Superintendent of the Sunday School and Deacon. He was also the church historian. Mr. Johnson died on February 21, 1998, three weeks prior to his 102nd birthday.

(Left) John Morton Leake, Jr. Great, Great, Great Grandson of Colonial Samuel and Sarah Johnson-Leake. *(Right)* Earnest Edward Lacey, Great, Great, Great Grandson of Joseph H. "FreeJoe" and Fanny Harris. Samuel Leake and Joseph H. "FreeJoe" Harris came to Shelby County, Tennessee from Goochland County, Virginia together in 1833.

Gray's Creek Missionary Baptist Church founded in February of 1843 by Joseph H. "FreeJoe" Harris, is the oldest active African-American church in Shelby County, Tennessee.

Documents

EXECUTOR'S BOND.

State of Tennessee,
SHELBY COUNTY.

WE, *Watt C Allen, James W. Allen, F B Haynes & C E Williams*

are bound to the State of Tennessee in the penalty of *Seven thousand & six hundred* Dollars.

Witness our hands and Seals, this *5* day of *August* 187 *5*

The Condition of this Obligation is such, That, whereas, the above bound *Watt C. Allen* _____ has been appointed Execut *or* of *Joseph Harris,* _____ deceased.

Now, if the said *Watt C. Allen* _____ shall well and truly perform and discharge all the duties and obligations which are or may be required of *him* by law, to be performed and discharged, as such Execut *or*, then this obligation shall be void; otherwise to be and remain in full force and virtue.

W C Allen [SEAL.]
James W. Allen [SEAL.]
F B Haynes [SEAL.]
C. E. Williams [SEAL.]

WITNESS, *James Reilly* CLERK.

By *Jno J Shea* D. C.

Approved by the Court *August* Term, 187 *6*

J C H Ray JUDGE.

Executor's Bond
August 5, 1875

101

COUNTY OF SHELBY. I do solemnly swear that we are the owners, in our own name, right and title, of the following property, subject to execution in Shelby County, after the payment of all just debts and encumbrances, described as follows:

I am the owner of 200 Acres of Land in 9th Civil District Shelby Co.

worth $5,000 _____ Dollars.

James H. Allen [SEAL.]

I am the owner of a one half interest in Lot No 10 of Sarah E Law's Subdivision in Shelby County Tenn.

worth $2,000 _____ Dollars.

J B Haynes [SEAL.]

I am the owner of 150 Acres of Land in 9th Civil District Shelby Co. & personal property

worth $1600 _____ Dollars.

C. E. Williams [SEAL.]

Sworn to and subscribed before me, this ___ day

of August 1875

James Reilly CLERK.

Jno J Shea D. C.

Memphis, Tenn. Thursday August 5 1875

In the matter of the
Last Will and Testament
of Joseph Harris Decd.
} In the Probate Court of
Shelby County Tennessee

This day was produced in open Court a paper
writing purporting to be the Last Will and
Testament of Joseph Harris Decd, for Probate.
Then came into Court C. E. Williams J. D.
Stewart and J. James subscribing witnesses
thereto, who first being duly sworn deposed
as follows, That the said Joseph Harris
acknowledged to them to have signed said
paper writing as his last Will and Testament
That they signed the same as attesting witnesses at his request and in his presence
And at the time of signing the same he
was of sound mind and memory, Where=
upon the said paper writing was admitted
to probate, as the last will and testament
of Joseph Harris Decd, and ordered to be
recorded in the Record of Wills of this Court,
Then came into Court James M. Crews
Cornelius Harris and Watt Allen executors
named and appointed in said Will. and the
said J. M. Crews and Cornelius Harris
waived their right and relinquished the same
as executors in behalf of Watt Allen,

The Presentation of Joseph "FreeJoe" Harris will (Probate Court)
August 5, 1875

Then

Came into Court Uball. C: Allen the Executive named in said will and entered into bond in the sum of Seven thousand Six hundred Dollars with James. W. Allen. T. B. Haynes and C. E. Williams as his sureties which bond having been seen and examined by the Court is approved. and he having qualified as by law required. It is ordered that Letters Testamentary issue to him accordingly.

John Schibler Admr of
No 974 Record No. 4   } Order Confirming Settlement
T. Peak decd

                         As recommend that this
Cause came on to be heard on the Settlement of said
_____ ___ and the Report of the ___

The Presentation of Joseph "FreeJoe" Harris will (Probate Court)
August 5, 1875 (cont.)

<u>TRANSCRIPTION</u>

Memphis, Tenn. Thursday   ⎞ AUGUST 5, 1875
In the matter of the   ⎟
Last will and testament   ⎬   IN THE PROBATE COURT
of Joseph Harris Dec'd   ⎠   SHELBY COUNTY TENNESSEE

This day was produced in open court a paper writing
purporting to be the last will and testament of Joseph
Harris dec'd for probate.

Then came into court C.E. Williams, J.D. Stewart and J.
James subscribing witnesses thereto, who first being duly
sworn deposed as follows. That the said Joseph Harris
acknowledged to them to have signed said proper writing as
his last will and testament. That they signed the same as
attesting witnesses at his request and in his presence and
at the time of signing the same he was of sound mind and
memory. Where upon the said proper writing was admitted to
probate as the last will and testament of Joseph Harris
dec'd, and ordered to be recorded in the record of wills of
the court.

Then came into court James M. Crews, Cornelius Harris and
Watt Allen executors named and appointed in said will and
the said J. M. Crews and Cornelius Harris waived their right
and relinguished the same as executors in behalf of Watt
Allen. Then came into court Watt C. Allen the executrix
named in said will and entered into bond in the sum of seven
thousand six hundred dollars with James W. Allen, F.B.
Haynes and C. E. Williams as his sureties which bond having
been seen and examined by the court is approved and he
having qualified as by law required. It is ordered that
letters testament any issue to him accordingly.

John Scheibler Admin of   ⎞
No 974 Record No 4   ⎬ Order confirming Settlement
F. Beck Dee   ⎠

The Presentation of Joseph "FreeJoe" Harris will (Probate Court)
August 5, 1875 (cont.)

1

To the Honorable Probate Court of Shelby County Tenn
The Undersigned Executor of Jo Harris decd Would
respectfully submit the following Inventory of all
the personal property of decd with 87 acres of Land
(which is to be sold by the Executor as directed in the
will of decd) to your Honorable Court.

Aug 5th/1875	Cash on hand	1945 32	
	{87 Acres of Land more or less valued at	870 00	
	Accounts to Amt of	6 00	Bad
	No Notes		
	Household & Kitchen furniture		
	Farming utensils Stock &c		
	3 Feather Beds & Covering $20.00	60 00	
	4 Bed Steads 3.00	12 00	
	1 Lounge 1.00 1 Spining Wheel 1.50	2 50	
	1 Book Case 3.00 1 Beaurean 6.00	9 00	
	2 Small Tables 1.25	2 50	
	1 Looking Glass 1.00 Andirons and Tongs 1.00	2 00	
	2 Bo Stidiards 1.00, 3 Tables 9.00	10 00	
	1 Safe and Table ware	5 00	
	1 Sausage Mill 1.00 2 Smoothing Irons 1.00	2 00	
	Buckets Jars Bole &c	2 00	
	1 Dz Chairs 3.00, 2 Bridles & Saddle 2.00	5 00	
	1 Truckle Bed & Fixtures	2 50	
	1 Cook Stove and Fixtures	10 00	
	3/4 Bbl Salt 1.50 / 50 Lb Bacon 12¢ 18.00	19 50	
	1 Spade & Shovel 2.00, Hoes & Cross Cut Saw 3.00	5 00	
	1 Grass Blade 1.00, Ax & Wedg 2.00	3 00	
	5 Set Plow Gear 1.00	5 00	
	3 Horses & 2 Mules 100.00	500 00	
	12 Plows and Stocks 2.00	24 00	
	Oats in Stack and house	8 00	
	1 Buggy and Harnifs	50 00	
		3540 32	

Inventory of Joseph "FreeJoe" Harris Assets (Probate Court)
August 17, 1875

Amt Brought forward		$840 32
2	Wagons 30.⁰⁰ $60.⁰⁰ 16 Bbl Corn 5.⁰⁰ $80.⁰⁰	140.00
3	Sithe Cradles 4.⁵⁰ / Trunk 1.⁵⁰	6 00
2500	℔ Lumber 1.⁵⁰	37 50
12	Head of Cattle 8.⁰⁰	96 00
14	" " Hogs 3.⁰⁰	42 00
80	Bu Wheat ,90.ᶜ	72 00
½	Bu Measure & Bbls	50
1	Wheat Fan	5 00
	Growing Crop valued at	40000
	$ 4339.32	

Joseph Harris
Dec⁴

2619 &

Thurston

W. C. Allen
Ex⁴ʳ

Filed Aug 17/75

James Kelly
Clerk

Entered Jany 8, 1876

Entered Inv book E
page 50
$1.25

Inventory of Joseph "FreeJoe" Harris Assets (Probate Court) cont.

Bartlett Tenn Aug 14th/877

Mr Cullins
    Dear Sir
            You will see in my Inventory
with the Estate of Jos Harris Decd 1 mule and
4 cows (or Cattle) are named more than was accounted
for in the Sale. You will see in the Marriage
Contract that the Decd gave his wife one horse
the widow prefured one of the mules which I
had bought in for her at $125.00 The two
Cows were valued at $18.00 Each. One other cow
died and the other belonged to one of the neighbors
If you think best you will please note the above
with my settlement and oblige Yours &c
                                    WC Allen

Sale of Property belonging to Estate of Jos. Harris deceased Sold Decr. 15th 1875 by W. C. Allen Ex.

Names	Article	Amt.
George Branch	1 Dining Table	$4.50
Stephen Pearce	1 Trundel Bed	50
John Lee	1 Small Table	55
"	1 Water Bucket	75
Robt Mathews	1 Ferkin	55
Widow Harris	1 Bed & Bedding	19.75
Jeff Jones Jr	1 Table Stand	2.00
" " "	1 Clock	1.25
Widow Mathews	1 Lounge & Matrass	1.70
George Branch	1 Book case	4.50
" "	1 Lot Bottles	25
Jeff Jones Jr	1 Beauro & Glass	7.00
John Redisard	1 Small Table	30
Charley Guy	1 Bed & Bedding	5.75
John Lee	1 " " "	4.95
Jim Price	1 Lantern	25
Robt Ford	1 Looking Glass	1.65
Albert Crawford	1 Reel	25
Geo. Branch	1 Saddle & Bridle	1.25
Widow Harris	4 Chairs	1.50
J. H. Cojer	½ Doz Chairs	1.90
Jeff Jones Sr	1½ Dz. Sacks	1.00
Geo. Branch	1½ Bu. Corn & Sack	1.30
" "	1 Feather Bed & Bedding	18.50
Jeff Jones Jr	1 Btl. Lime	1.00
Geo. Branch	1 " " Remnant	.75 83.45

Sale of Joseph "FreeJoe" Harris Property (Probate Court)
December 15, 1875

Robt. Ford	1 Lamp	8 .10
Geo. Branch	1 Churn & Jar	1.50
Wm. Harris	1 Large Jar	.80
Frank Leake	Table & Contents	.75
Jeff. Jones Jr	1 Mirror	.50
Geo. Branch	1 Kettle & Jar	2.10
Widow Harris	1 Jar & Bucket	75
Jeff. Jones Sr	1 Sausage Mill	3.10
Stephen Price	1 Lot Pans	75
John Lee	1 Lot "	40
Nelson Leake	5 Smoothing Irons	1.35
Charley Guy	1 Large Table	2.10
Stephen Price	1 Cup Board	.50
Geo. Branch	1 Coal oil Can & Bottles	.30
" "	1 Safe & contents	8.00
" "	1 Table cloth	.65
" "	1 Tray & Coffee Mill	.50
Widow Harris	1 Tray	.50
Jeff Jones Jr.	1 Table & contents	.60
Charley Guy	1 Table Skillet & Pan	.10
Geo. Branch	1 Stove & Fixtures	4.85
Widow Harris	1 Water Bucket	15
John Lee	1 Large Skillet	2.10
Widow Harris	1 Large Cup Board	25
Stephen Pearce	1 Pot Shovel & Kettle	.50
Widow Harris	1 Kettle & Hooks	.75
Jeff Jones Jr.	1 Large Pot	1.10
Chas. Williams	1 Four horse Wagon & 2 Beds	25.00 60.05

**Sale of Joseph "FreeJoe" Harris Property (Probate Court)
December 15, 1875 (cont.)**

Name	Item	Price
Geo. Branch	1 Cradle No 1	1.05
Peter Leake	1 " " 2	1.30
Jeff Jones Jr.	1 Grass Blade	1.50
Frank Taylor	1 Hide	20
Oswell Harris	1 Plow & Shovel	55
Geo. Branch	1 Bull Tongue Plow	2.05
Robt. Ford	1 Shovel Plow	3.00
Charley Guy	1 " "	2.00
Jos Lewis	1 Cotton Scraper	1.00
Albert Slaughter	Steelyard Knife & Iron	1.70
Jeff Jones Jr.	1 Lot Tools	2.00
Geo Branch	1 Broad Ax & 2 Wedges	1.25
J. D. Godley	2 Turning Plows	3.25
Charley Guy	1 Harrow & Plow	2.35
Albert Crawford	1 Turning Plow & Harrow	.88
Jeff Jones Sr.	1 & Harrow	1.30
John Mebane	1 Cross Cut Saw	2.50
Robt. Ford	3 Hoes	.40
Geo. Branch	1 Spade & Shovel	1.95
Widow Harris	1 Turning Plow, Shovel & Hoe	5.00
N. J. Justice	1 Brindle Cow	12.75
" " "	2 Heifers	10.00
Geo Branch	1 Steer & Heifer	9.50
C. C. Williams	2 Small Steers	4.50
N. J. Justice	1 White Cow	7.00
Geo. Branch	1 Large Spotted Barrow	8.50
" "	1 Spotted Sow	10.50
Temp Redd	1 Sow & Small Pigs	3.75
Richmond Bennett	2 Hogs, 1st Choice	8.25 10.70

Sale of Joseph "FreeJoe" Harris Property (Probate Court)
December 15, 1875 (cont.)

111

Name	Item	Price
J. W. Allen	2 Hogs 2nd Choice	5.00
Robt. Ford	" " 3rd "	3.05
John Mehane	4 " 4th "	12.50
J. W. Allen	8 Shoats 2.05 each	16.40
H. L. Priddy	4 Pigs @ 1.30 each	5.20
Thos. Richmond	4 " " .80 each	3.20
Ben Askew	1 Buggy & Harness	17.00
Geo. Branch	1 – 2 Horse wagon	20.50
J. W. Alley	2000 Lbs Fodder 55 pr C.	11.00
Geo. Branch	2069 " " 55 "	11.38
N. J. Justice	1 Stack Oats	5.00
Geo. Branch	26 Bbls Corn 2.00 pr bbl	40.00
Widow Harris	15 " " 2.05 "	30.75
Ben Askew	10 " " 2.00 "	20.00
Green McSpadden	2½ Bbls Corn 2.05 pr bbl	5.12
Jeff Jones Jr.	5 " " 2.05 "	10.25
Dr J. C. Ellicott	13½ " " 2.00 "	27.00
Geo. Branch	37 " " 1.95 "	72.00
Chas Williams	20 " " 1.90 "	38.00
N. J. Justice	1 Plow, Harrow & Corn Sheller	05
Geo. Branch	1 Bay Horse	51.50
" "	1 Chesnut mare	57.00
Jeff Jones Jr	1 Bay Colt	40.00
Ben Askew	1 " mule Large	42.00
Geo. Branch	1 Set Wagon Harness	5.00
Charley Guy	2 Collars & pr Gear	1.40
Red. Hall	Grind Stone Saddle &½ Harness	.80
Robt Ford	1 Lot Gear	1.55

Sale of Joseph "FreeJoe" Harris Property (Probate Court)
December 15, 1875 (cont.)

112

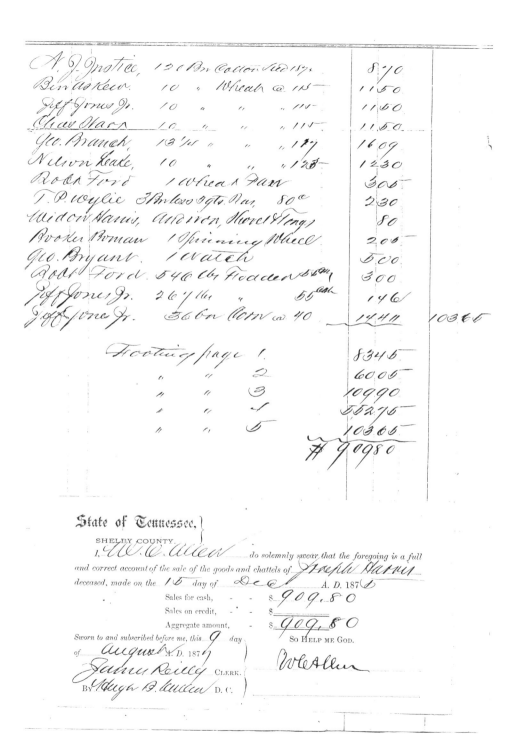

A. J. Justice,	12 Bu Cotton Seed 15¢	870	
Ben Askew,	10 " Wheat @ 115	1150	
Jeff Jones Jr.	10 " " " 115	1160	
Elias Harn	10 " " " 115	1150	
Geo. Branch,	13½ " " " 127	1609	
Nelson Leake,	10 " " " 125	1230	
Robt Ford	1 Wheat Fan	305	
T. P. Wylie	3 Bu less 2 qts Rye, 80¢	230	
Widow Harris,	and iron, Hoes & Tongs	80	
Brooks Bowman	1 Spinning Wheel	200	
Geo. Bryant.	1 Watch	500	
Robt Ford.	546 lbs Fodder 55¢/cwt	300	
Jeff Jones Jr.	267 lbs " 55¢ cash	146	
Jeff Jones Jr.	36 Bu Corn @ 40	1441	10365

Footing page 1.	8345	
" " 2	6005	
" " 3	10990	
" " 4	55275	
" " 5	10365	
	$ 90980	

Sale of Joseph "FreeJoe" Harris Property (Probate Court)
December 15, 1875 (cont.)

Whereas on the 6th day of February 1878, I, Walter
C. Allen Executor of Joseph Harris deceased did
make and execute a warranty deed to Peter Leake
Joseph Lewis, Frank Leake, and Rhoda Green
which Deed is recorded in the Registers office of
Shelby County Tennessee to which reference is
here made Book 127, Page 530. And whereas in
said deed one of the parties as above was named
Peter Leake when it should be Peter Harris, Now
therefore for and in consideration of the prem-
ises and for the purpose of correcting said error
I Walter C. Allen Executor of Joseph Harris
deceased do hereby Quit Claim unto the said
Peter Harris named in said deed as Peter
Leake all right title claim and interest that
I may have had as the Executor of Jos. Harris
in and to the before mentioned land,
Witness my hand and seal this 6th day
of April 1880.

                        Walter C. Allen
                    Executor of Jos. Harris
                            Decd.

State of Tennessee
Shelby County Personally appeared before
me Jno. J. Shea Deputy Clerk of the County
Court of said County Walter C. Allen Executor
of Jos. Harris dec'd the within named bar-
gainer with whom I am personally acquainted,
and who acknowledged that he executed
the within instrument for the purposes
therein contained,
      Witness my hand at Office this 6 day
of April A. D. 1880.

            Jno. J. Shea,
                Deputy Clerk

State of Tennessee
Shelby County The foregoing Instrument
with Clerk's certificate was filed in my office

Peter Leake was Peter Harris

**Note: Peter was the manservant on the Samuel Leake plantation and
it was assumed that his name was Leake.**

To the Hon. Jacob S Galloway, Judge of the Probate court of Shelby county State of Tennessee

The undersigned petitioners respectfully ~~submit to your~~ ~~honor that~~ Jeff Jones late of the 8th district of County ~~settled above~~ died about 3 years ago intestate and in possession of about 93 acres of Land in the above district _and a small amount of personal property of about $50.00_ He left the following heirs viz James Jones, Jeff X Jones jr Emma Harris, Medicus X Jones Callie Lewis & Phoebia Johnson. all of whom are residents of this County and state except Emma Harris and Phoeba Johnson who reside in Kalamazoo Michigan Said land is not susceptible of division and we respectfully pray that J. S. McGinley be appointed administrator to ~~sum~~ up said estate and do all things needful to give each legatee or heir his or her respective share

Real Estate (Probate Court) of Jeff Jones

The children of Jefferson M. and Adeline "Lettie" Jones petition the court concerning 93 acres of land.

Note: Two of the children lived in Kalamazoo, Michigan.

115

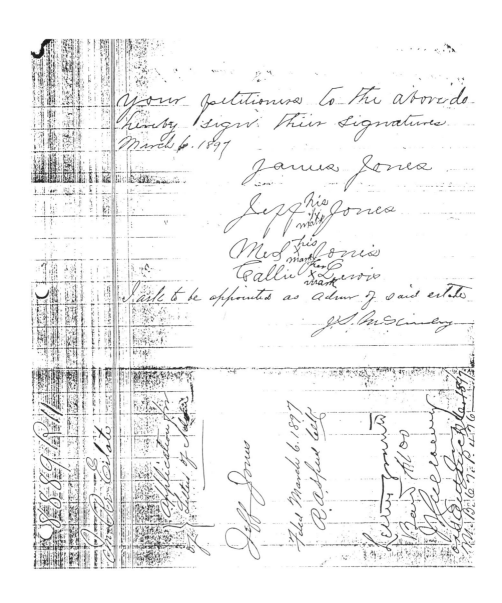

Your petitioners to the above do hereby sign their signatures.
March 6. 1897

James Jones

Jeff *his* *mark* Jones

Med *his* *mark* Jones

Callie *her* X *mark* Lewis

I ask to be appointed as admr of said estate

J.S. McGinley

Application for Letters of Administration

Jeff Jones Estate

Jeff Jones

Filed March 6. 1897
D. A. Head Clk.

Letters granted
Bond $150.00

M.D. 16 P. 457 6

Real Estate (Probate Court) of Jeff Jones (cont.)

116

State of Tennessee, }
SHELBY COUNTY   } ss.

I, B. J. DUNAVANT, Clerk of the Probate Court of this County, do hereby certify that the foregoing

Four (4)---------------------pages contain a full, true and exact copy of the

Last Will and Testament of Joseph Harris, Deceased

-------------- Will Book 6 page 548

e same appears of record or on file in---------

of this office.

IN TESTIMONY WHEREOF, I have hereunto set my hand and affixed the seal of said Court, at office,

in the City of Memphis, this 9th day of July 19 82

B. J. DUNAVANT, Clerk

By _____ D. C.

P-C-C 314-73A

The Will of Joseph "FreeJoe" Harris

On May 9, 1873, Joseph "FreeJoe" Harris completed his will and it
was filed in Shelby county, Tennessee.

117

I, Joseph Harris, in the Eighth Civil
District Of Shelby County And State
of Tennessee - a farmer, being of Sound
d Mind, memory, and understanding,
do make and publish this, as my
last Will and Testament; hereby
revoking and making void all
others, by me at any time made.

First: I direct that my funeral
expenses and all my debts be paid
as soon after my death as possible,
out of any moneys that I may
die possessed of, or may first come
into the hands of my executors.
Secondly: I give
and devise unto my daughter, Martha
Branch, wife of George Branch, and
unto my son Cornelius, each fifty
acres of land (making one-hundred
acres) beginning at the Eastern boundary of my tract of land, upon which
I now reside; said tract lying and
being, a part in the Eighth, and a
part in the Ninth Civil District,
of the County of Shelby and State of
Tennessee; said One hundred acres
given to my above named daughter
Martha, and Son Cornelius, must

The Will of Joseph "FreeJoe" Harris (cont.)

118

include my present residence and
all adjoining out houses.

Thirdly: I give and
devise unto my daughter Lettie
Jones, wife of Jefferson M Jones, Fifty
acres of land of my said tract—
and unto my daughter Mary Ford,
wife of Robert Ford, Fifty acres of my
said tract.— And should my wife
Milly, be living at my death I
give and devise unto her Thirty
acres of land of my said tract—

Fourthly: I will and
direct that the remaining Eighty—
Seven acres of land of my said tract,
be the same more or less.— Shall be
sold by my executors, after a proper
and sufficient public notice,— at public
out=cry to the highest and best bidder
for one third Cash, and the balance
payable in one and two years, with
interest and approved security. And
I give and bequeath unto my son Peter
Harris, my daughter Rhoda and
Virginia (and also one equal share
to be divided equally between my two
grand children) the children of my
daughter Maria) equally, share and

The Will of Joseph "FreeJoe" Harris (cont.)

Share alike.

Fifthly; I give and bequeath unto my son James Harris, and unto my daughter Sarah ten dollars each.

Sixthly; I give and bequeath unto my daughters, Martha, Mary and Lettie, and Son Cornelius, equally; that is share and share alike all money or moneys that may be on hand at my death after all my debts shall have been paid.

Seventhly; Should there not be money enough on hand at my death to settle all my debts, I direct that my executors shall sell at public Sale, after legal notice, such personal property as they may deem advisable, and with the proceeds pay off all my debts and I give and bequeath the remainder of all my personal property of every description whatever, unto my daughters Martha, Mary and Lettie, and Son Cornelius equally, that is share and share alike.

Lastly; I do hereby nominate and appoint James M. Carney my Son Cornelius and Matt Allen my executors.

The Will of Joseph "FreeJoe" Harris (cont.)

In testimony whereof I do, to this my
Will Set my hand and seal,
this the 9th day of May one—
thousand eight hundred and Seventy—
three. a. D. 1873

Joseph Harris Seal

Signed sealed and published in our
presence, and we have Subscribed
our names hereto in the presence
of the testator. this the 9th day of
May 1873 One—thousand eight—hund—
red and Seventy three a. D. 1873.,

C. E. Williams
J. D. Stewart.
E. J. Isom

CONFIRMED BY THE PROBATE COURT AT ITS AUGUST TERM 1875 AND
ORDERED TO BE RECORDED

RECORDED AUGUST 17th 1875

The Will of Joseph "FreeJoe" Harris (cont.)

121

[Handwritten deed, largely illegible]

Know all men by these presents that I Samuel Leake of the county of Shelby State of Tennessee for and in consideration of three hundred dollars the receipt of one hundred and ... dollars part thereof hereby acknowledge, hath this day bargained and sold and do by these presents bargain and sell unto Joseph Harris a free man of color all my right title Claim and interest in two negroes, Fanny the wife of said Joseph Harris and her child Virginia, and to his heirs and assigns forever — And the said Samuel Leake hereby binds himself his heirs and assigns to warrant and defend to the said Joseph Harris ...

I am Leake

[Witness and acknowledgment text largely illegible]

The Purchase of the Family

On November 14, 1834, Joseph purchased his wife, Fanny and a daughter Virginia out of slavery for the sum total of $300.00 from Samuel Leake. Joseph came to Shelby county, Tennessee as a free man but his wife Fanny and the children, Peter, James, Susan (Sucky), Adeline (Lettie) and Virginia came as slaves of Samuel Leake.

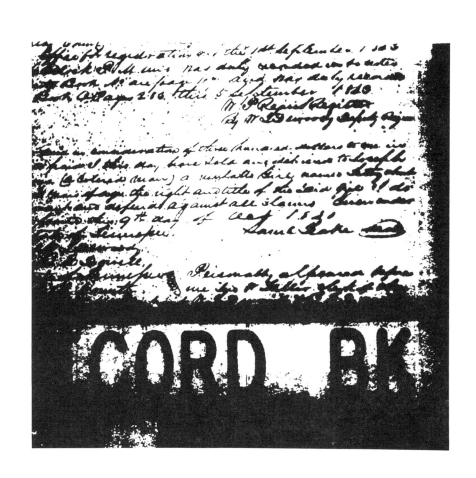

The Purchase of the Family

On October 9, 1840, Joseph purchase his daugther Adeline (Lettie) out of slavery for the sum total of $300.00 from Samuel Leake.

123

For and in consideration of three hundred dollars to me in
hand paid I this day have sold and delivered to Joseph
Harris (a colored man) a mulatto girl named Letty about
nine years of age the right and title of the said girl I do
warrant and defend against all claims. Given under my hand
and seal this 9th day of Oct. 1840.

Samuel Leake se

The Purchase of the Family (cont.)

Know all men by these presents that we Bennett Bagby & Frances C Bagby of the State of Tennessee and County of _____ of the first part for and in consideration of the sum of Nine hundred Dollars lawful money of the United States to me in hand paid, at or before the sealing and delivery of these presents by Joseph Harris of the same place of the second part, the receipt whereof is hereby acknowledged have bargained and sold and by these presents to grant and convey unto the said party of the second part, his executors, administrators and assigns, One negro woman named Sukey twenty eight years of age _____ a Slave for life, to have and to hold the same unto the said party of the second part, his executors, administrators and assigns forever, and I do for myself my heirs, executors & administrators covenant and agree to and with the said part of the second part to Warrant and defend the Sale of the said negro hereby sold unto the said party of the second part his executors, administrators and assigns against all and every person or persons whomsoever. In Witness Whereof _____ _____ hand and _____

RECORD BK
24   199

The Purchase of Family

In June of 1856, Joseph "FreeJoe" Harris purchased his daughter Susan (Sucky) out of slavery for the sum total of $900.00 from Bennett and Frances C. Bagby, the son-in-law and daughter of Samuel and Sarah Leake.

125

Eight hundred and fifty six
Sealed and delivered
in the presence of
Frances Baugh as to B. Bagby
Erasmus J. Rose
P. S. Ellis as to C. Bagby
John H. Hanson D.C.
June 5th 1856

Bennett Bagby   (Seal)

Frances C. Bagby   (Seal)

State of Tennessee } Before me John P. Trezevant Clerk of the County
County of Shelby } Court of said County personally appeared
Frances Baugh & P. S. Ellis two of the Subscribing Witnesses to
the foregoing Bill of Sale who being duly sworn do say that they
acquainted with Bennett Bagby one of the bargainers to the foregoing
Bill of Sale and that he acknowledged executing the same for the
purposes therein contained in their presence. Also personally appeared
Frances C. Bagby, the other bargainor to me personally known and
acknowledged executing the said Bill of Sale freely willingly and understandingly without compulsion on the part of her husband. Done
at Office June 5th 1856.

John P. Trezevant Clk.
By John H. Hanson D.C.

State of Tennessee } This Bill of Sale was filed in my office for
Shelby County } Registration on the 6th day of June 1856 at
8 O'clock A.M. and as noted in Note Book No. 3 page 210. And
was duly Recorded on the 20th day of the same month.

Henry Lake Register

The Purchase of Family (cont.)

126

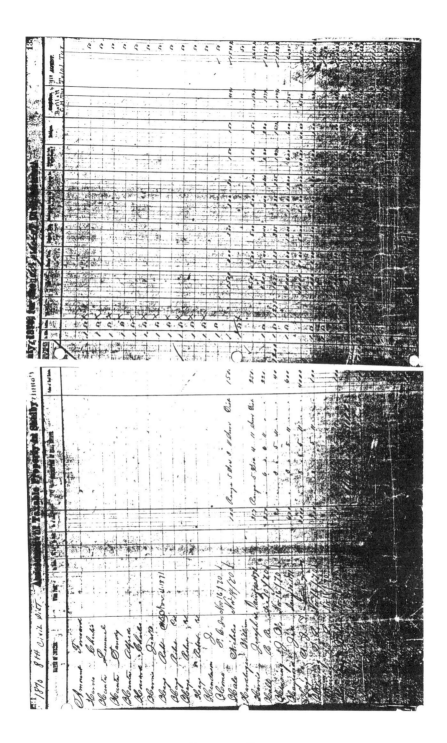

Property Taxes
The taxes paid by Joseph "FreeJoe" Harris on February 10, 1871.

1872

NAMES OF OWNERS, OR TO WHOM LISTED	WHEN PAID			No. of ACRES		DESCRIPTION OF REAL ESTATE

Property Taxes

The taxes paid by Joseph "FreeJoe" Harris on February 6, 1873.

Stagecoach Line

In May of 1845, Joseph "FreeJoe" Harris established a stagecoach line that ran from Bolivar, Tennessee to Memphis, Tennessee.

The Docket Book of Transactions

A copy of this page of transactions was provided by the Goochland County, VA. courthouse in 1984. The arrows which identify the transaction were made by a clerk at the courthouse. Joseph Harris was emancipated on September 5, 1832, book 29, page 370.

130

Know all men by these presents that I John Harris senr of the
County of Goochland & State of Virginia, have manumitted, emancipated and set
free, and by these presents do manumit, emancipate and set free,
a negro man slave named Joseph and commonly called Joseph
Harris, who was born my property, and I do hereby deliver him, the
said Joseph Harris to be entirely liberated from slavery, and entitled
to all the rights and privileges of a free person with which it is in
my power to vest him – He the said Joseph Harris hereby emancipated
is a man of yellow complexion about five feet seven inches high
and was thirty seven years of age on the 12th day of July last.
In testimony whereof I have hereunto set my hand and seal this
my and this 5 day of September eighteen hundred and thirty two

                                        his
                                John + Harris and seal
                                        mark

Signed, sealed & delivered
in the presence of
David W Miller

In Goochland County Court Clerks Office 5th September 1832.
      This Deed of Emancipation was this day presented to me
and acknowledged by John Harris senr to be his act
on the said Office and admitted to record – Teste ... Maston H ...

The Emancipation of Joseph "FreeJoe" Harris

QUIT CLAIM DEED

KNOW ALL MEN BY THESE PRESENTS, That......Virge A. Lewis, unmarried, of Cleveland Ohio,

for and in consideration of......One ($1.00) and No/100 - - - -

.......DOLLARS,

do hereby bargain, sell, remise, release, quit claim and convey unto......Bernice Lacey, of Chicago, Illinois.

the following described real estate located in......, County of Shelby, State of Tennessee, to-wit:

PARCEL I:
In the 9th civil district (as of 1908) of Shelby County, and described in a deed from the Circuit Clerk to W. T. Horton, in Book 338, Page 109, and in a deed from W. T. Horton to Joe Lewis (also known as Joseph Lewis) recorded in Book 444, Page 406, both in the Register's Office of Shelby County, Tennessee:
  Bounded on the North by Green, on the east by Ford, on the south by Williams, and on the west by Lewis, containing 19 Acres;

PARCEL II:
Described in the deed from Peter Harris, Frank Leake and Rhoda Green to Joseph Lewis (also known as Joe Lewis) recorded in Book 129, Page 538 of the Register's Office of Shelby County, Tennessee:
  Being Lot No. 3, beginning at the Northwest corner of Lot No. 2, and running south 49 chains and 65 links to a stake persimmon pointer; thence west 4 chains to a stake in the creek Black gum pointer; thence North 49 chains and 65 links to a stake in the south boundary line of Lot No. 1; thence east 4 chains to the beginning, containing 19.8 acres, and being Lot No. 3 of a plat of survey made by N. L. Owen, Surveyor, Feby. 5th, 1876, and the center lot a tract containing 81.17 acres bought by all the parties to this deed from W. C. Allen, Executor of Joseph Harris, Dec'd., and recorded in Book 129, Page 530, in the records of said county.
Joe Lewis and Joseph Lewis are the same party, he having died in about 1918 at Eads, Tenn., intestate, and grantor being his grandson.
I (We) do hereby warrant the title herein conveyed against the lawful claims of all persons claiming the same by, through or under me (us), but not further or otherwise.

IN TESTIMONY WHEREOF I (We) have executed this instrument this the 13th day of.....April June, 19 61

Maurice Tamarkin   x *Virge A Lewis*
                                         Virge A. Lewis

Ohio   Cuyahoga
STATE OF TENNESSEE, COUNTY OF SHELBY
  Before me, a Notary Public in and for said State and County, duly commissioned and qualified, personally appeared......
.......Virge A. Lewis, Unmarried,
to me known to be the person......described in and who executed the foregoing instrument, and acknowledged that......he......executed the same as......his......free act and deed.
  WITNESS my hand and Notarial Seal at office this 13th day of......April June 19 61

MAURICE TAMARKIN, Notary Public
My Commission Expires Oct. 6, 1961
Cuyahoga County

Maurice Tamarkin
Notary Public

My commission expires:......

State Tax......$ 15
Clerk's Fee......$ STATE OF TENNESSEE,}   Reg. No.

Quit Claim Deed

This is the document that my mother, Bernice Earnestine Lewis-Lacey summon me to her house to see. This is the property referred to in the fourth paragraph of the will of Joseph "FreeJoe" Harris.

Dogwood Village on highway 64 in Eads, Tennessee occupies this property today. A marker indicates that the property was donated by the descendants of Joseph and Callie F Lewis, my great grandparents. Joseph "FreeJoe" Harris was the grandfather of Joseph and Callie F. Lewis who in addition to being husband and wife were also first cousins.

AGRICULTURAL CENSUS
1870

8th Civil Dist

Joseph Harris

Acres of Land	
Improved	60
Woodland	200
Primary Cash Value	$2,600
Value of Farming Implements and Machinery	$15
Horses	2
Mules and Asses	2
Milk Cows	4
Other Cattle	5
Swine	20
Value of All The Stock	$600
Wheat, Bushels of	90
Indian Corn, Bushels of	350
Oats, Bushels of	50
Cotton, Bales of 400 Lbs	2
Establish of All Crops and Livestock	$700

The Agricultural Census of 1870
What Joseph "FreeJoe" Harris grew and raised on his farms.

In the name of God, Amen: I, Richard
Leake, of the county of Shelby and State of
Tennessee, being of lawful age and sound
mind, do make and publish this my last will
and testament, hereby revoking all other
wills made heretofore by me.

1st. I direct, that my funeral and burial
expenses, and all my just and legal debts
be paid as soon after my death as possible.

2nd. That, after such expenses and debts are
paid, an equal distribution of all my
property be made to each of my children, viz. Maricela A. Woolson, Indiana
H. Lenow, Thomas C. Leake, Elisha
H. Leake, Joseph E. Leake, children
of my first wife, and Stern C. Lancaster, Richard W. Leake, Lucy V. Leake, &
Marcella C. Leake, children of my last
wife, taking into account the property
and money already given to any of them.

3rd. That in such distribution, the negro
property, that came into my possession by
my first wife, be loaned to my first
wife's children, and the negro property
that came by my last wife be loaned to
my last wife's children, making the equ-
ality in distribution from my other negro property. The following property came
by my first wife viz. Maria and her children, Eliza and her children, and Joe. The
following by my last wife viz. Matilda and
her children; Nancy and her children, and
Lucy and her children.

4th. That in distributing my property to my
children, I loan it to them during their natural
lives and at their death to be given to the lawful heirs
of their bodies. But if any of them die without a lawful heir of their body, then to revert
back and be divided equally among my grandchil-

The Will of Richard Leake

**March 29, 1850, Joseph "FreeJoe" Harris appears in the
probate records of Richard Leake, a plantation owner
in Shelby county, Tennessee.**

134

dren.

5th I direct that my daughter Mariella J. Woodson must be held accountable for a negro woman named Eliza aged 24 years, a negro girl Susan aged 13 years and a negro girl, Jane, aged 4 or 5 years an a negro boy, Abram 11 months old, to be valued as such negroes in age and quality, may be valued at the general division of my negro property. She must also account for one horse, one bed and furniture and two cows and calves, valued at one hundred and ten dollars.

6th My daughter Indiana H. Lewis must account for a negro girl named Frances aged 8 years to be valued likewise as before directed. And also for one horse, one bed and furniture, one cow and two young oxen valued at one hundred and thirty five dollars.

7th My daughter Ann E. Lancaster must account for one bed and furniture valued at fifty dollars. & for one hundred dollars in hand to Dr. La

8th I direct that my younger children, viz. Richard W. Leake, Lucy. V. Leake and Marcella C. Leake must be supported and educated, until they become 18 years of age or marry, from my general estate, by each legatees being bound to pay over to my executors, annually, equally, an amount sufficient for such purpose.

9th The dividend accruing to my son Thomas O. Leake must be placed in the hands of a trustee, to be managed to the best advantage for his support and emolument.

10. My real estate, I direct to be equally divided, and loaned to my children, above named during their natural life, and then given to my grand children: Provided however, that my children shall have the power to sell each their portion of real estate, at any time they may choose

The Will of Richard Leake (cont.)

135

but shall invest the money accruing from said real estate in other lands, for my grand children.

11. I hereby appoint my son E. H. Leake Doct. W. F. Lancaster and Mr. James Lenow executors of this my last will and testament.

In testimony whereof I have hereunto set my hand and affixed my seal this 24th day of Nov. 1848.

Rich'd Leake (L.S.)

Attest:

Samuel A. Leake

Jas W. Leake

Sarah Leake

John Nobles

Proven at July Term 1850 And Recorded July 6th 1850

Wm L Dewoody Clerk

The Will of Richard Leake (cont.)

136

*An Inventory of the personal
property of Richard Leake deceased*

Names of Slaves	Ages	
Abram	84	Infirm
George	55	List of Men
Humphry	55	
Joseph	37	
Nelson	30	
James	29	
Marshall	21	
Dolly	47	List of Women
Moriah	40	
Rhodia	35	
Nancy	28	
Lucy	25	
Mary	25	
Moriah Jr.	13	List of girls
Harriet	11	
Lydia	4	
Edmonia	3	
America	2	
Willie Ann	1½	
Patience	8 Mo.	
Henry	16	List of Boys
Robert	15	
Mat	11	
William	9	
Scott	6	
David	6	
Frank	5	
Thomas	4	
Morgan	2	

The Will of Richard Leake (cont.)

137

Stock

Horses 4 —
Mules 4 — — —
Cattle young & old about 25 heads
Stock Hogs ... about 25 heads
Pork Hogs ,, 55 heads

One Carriage, Buggy and Waggon
Farming Utensils, Saws Axes &c
Black Smith's Tools
One Wheat & Oat Fan
One Corn & Frost Mill
Beds 6 & bed Furniture
One Beauro Secretary & Cupboard
One Clock, Large Mirror, & other small furniture
Kitchen Furniture & other things
Such as old ploughs; Cart Wheels
boxes, barrels, & other trinkets

Notes & Accounts

One Note of $150.00 on Joseph Harris, Good Claim
and due the first day of Feby. 1851

Note on John James of $20.00 ~~Due 25th of Decr~~
And due 25th of Decr, 1850 Good Claim

Constable; Receipt for an Acc.] of $2.00 on
G. M. Bowers Deed) Due Jany. 1st 1840 Good Claim ~~Doubtful~~

Due Bill of $2.19 on Jn Thompson
Due Jany 1850 — Good Claim

The Will of Richard Leake (cont.)

138

An Acc[t] on James Gray $1.82 cr. on same
$1.15 leaving 67 cents due, Jany 1st 1847, doubtful

Two Notes on Joshua Sturges $30.62 each
First note due 25" Decr 1845. Cr. by $43. 00
Second note due 25" Decr 1846. Cr. by $30. 00
The two notes on Sturgess are bad claims

Stock in Plank Road $1000, Not Paid,

and of the [illegible] 1847 Sure claim
An Acc[t] on J W Boyster $9. 00, out of date
Due the Estate from John Nobles $15. 82. Good
The Estate due John Nobles $29. 79 [illegible] "
Constable Receipt for the collection of $03.00
due Feb 1842 $75.00 of which Good
Note on Walter Allen $67.85 cts due
one day after date ~ claim Good
Note on Hodges & Hallum $56.31 Due one day after date Good
The above is a true & perfect Inventory of all
the goods & Chattels rights & credits of the
said Richd. Leake deceased which have come
to my hands possession or knowledge or the
hands of any other person for me to the best
of my knowledge and belief
This 7th day of October 1830
Sworn to in open Court William G Lancaster Executor
October 7. 1830
        Wm L Dunwody Clk
        Recorded October 21. 1830
            Wm L Dunwody Clk

The Will of Richard Leake (cont.)

I, Samuel Leake, of the county of Shelby, and State of Tennessee, being of sound mind and memory, and considering the uncertainty of this life, do, therefore, make this my last will and testament, hereby revoking all former will by me made; First, after all my just and legal debts are paid and discharged, I dispose of the residue of my estate both real and personal as follows. viz: I lend to my beloved wife during her natural life, all that portion of land on which I now live, lying North of the main road leading from Memphis to Somerville, and that portion, South of said road, lying between said road and the land I recently sold to Wm. R. Watkins, running a line, direct from the North West corner of the land sold to said Watkins to the South East corner of Joseph Harris's fifty acres, on which he formerly lived: I also lend her my servants, Armistead, Joe, Rhoda and her five children, Maria and her two youngest children, and at her death, I direct that the dispose of all of said property to any or all of my children as she may choose, provided however that my son Edward C. Leake shall have, at her death, that portion of the land loaned to her lying south

The Will of Samuel Leake

In the will of Samuel Leake, Joseph and some of his children are referenced.

of the main road from Memphis to Somerville, and two hundred and fifty acres of that portion lying north of said road, having the road for its Southern boundary, and extending north for complement. I also give to my beloved wife in fee simple, my Mansion vant Peter, my carriage and two mules usually worked thereto. Secondly. I give to my two daughters Lucy Jane, and Virginia M. each one thousand dollars, and to my son Elisha M. five hundred dollars, which legacies are given as equivalents to property heretofore given to my other children, except as to my son Edward C. Leake, who is to receive as his equivalent that portion of the land hereinbefore described lying South of the main road, as hereinbefore provided. Thirdly. I direct that the residue of my estate both real and personal be equally divided between my the following named children, viz. Frances C. Bagby, Elisha M. Leake, Virginius Leake, Sarah S. Mosby, Martha E. Moseley, Lucy Jane Leake, Virginia M. Leake and my son Edward C. Leake, in personal or negro property only, he having been provided for in real estate: And my daughter Frances C. Bagby and my son Virginius Leake must each be held accountable in said division each for the sum of six hundred dollars for lands heretofore given to them.

The Will of Samuel Leake (cont.)

Fourthly. The legacies left to my daugh-
I give to them, for their own separate use
and benefit, in no wise to be subject to
claim, control, or liabilities of their husban-
ds present or future. The legacies left to my
son Elisha M. Leake, I lend to him during his natural life, in no wise to be
subject to his present or future liabilities, except as to the interest or profits thereto accruing by proper use and management, and at his death to be given to my grand
son, Walenstein Leake.

Finally: I constitute and appoint, my
beloved wife, My son, Virginius Leake,
and my son-in-law Samuel Mosby, my
executors to this my last will and testament.   In testimony whereof I hereunto subscribe my name and affix my seal
this 22nd of December, A.D. one thousand eigh-
t hundred and fifty five.

Sam'l. Leake {seal}

Attest
S. A. Leake
Wm. B. Watkins   +
J. W. Hooke   x

Proven at January Term 1856 and
Recorded on the 10th January, 1856
                John B. Tremant Clerk
             By John A. Harrison D.C.

The Will of Samuel Leake (cont.)

142

The Census of 1850

The family of Joseph "FreeJoe" Harris as shown in the United States census.

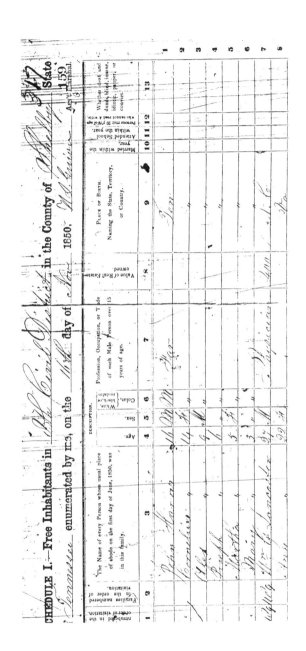

The Census of 1850 (cont.).

144

AGRICULTURAL CENSUS
1850

8th Civil Dist

Joseph Harris

Acres of Land	
Improved	35
Unemproved	65
Cash Value of Farm	$900
Value of Farming Implements and Machinery	$60
Horses	3
Asses and Mules	1
Milch Cows	3
Other Cattle	1
Swine	25
Value of Live Stock	$187
Indian Corn, Bushels of	200
Oats, Bushels of	50
Ginned Cotton, Bales of 400 Lbs Each	12
Wool, IBS of	20
Sweet Potatoes, Bush of	100
Butter, IBS of	180
Hay, Tons of	3
Beeswax and Honey, IBS of	40
Value of Home-made Manufactures	$40
Value of Animals Slaughtered	$120

The Agricultural census of 1850

This record show what Joseph "FreeJoe" Harris grew and raised on his farms.

AGRICULTURAL CENSUS
1860
8TH Civil Dist

Joseph Harris

Acres of Land	
Improved	50
Unemproved	217
Cash Value of Farm	$2,340
Value of Farming Implements and Machinery	$150
Horses	2
Asses and Mules	3
Milch Cows	3
Other Cattle	10
Swine	20
Value of Live Stock	$645
Wheat, Bushels of	50
Peas and Beans, Bushels of	5
Irish Potatoes, Bushels of	20
Sweet Potatoes, Bushels of	50
Butter, IBS of	100
Indian Corn, Bushels of	500
Ginned Cotton, Bales of 400 Lbs Each	5
Value of Animals Slaughtered	$50

The Agricultural census of 1860
What Joseph "FreeJoe" Harris grew and raised on his farms.

146

147

Inquiries numbered 7, 16, and 17 are not to be asked in respect to infants. Inquiries numbered 11, 12, 15, 16, 17, 19, and 20 are to be answered (if at all) merely by an affirmative mark, as /.

SCHEDULE 1.—Inhabitants in _8th Civil District_, in the County of _Shelby_, State of _Tenn_, enumerated by me on the _22_ day of _August_, 1870.

Post Office: _Shelby_

J. M. Bannum, Ass't Marshal.

		The name of every person whose place of abode on the first day of June, 1870, was in this family.	Age	Sex	Color	Profession, Occupation, or Trade of each person, male or female.	Value of Real Estate	Value of Personal Estate	Place of Birth, naming State or Territory of U. S.; or the Country, if of foreign birth.							Whether deaf and dumb, blind, insane, or idiotic.		
1	2	3	4	5	6	7	8	9	10	11	12	13	14	15	16	17	18	19	20
X	X	Harris Wm	20	M	B				Tenn					/	/				
		" Alice	19	F	B				"						/				
		" Sarah	16	F	B				"					/	/				
		" John	13	M	B				"					/	/				
		" Luella	11	F	B				"					/	/				
		" Joe	7	M	B				"										
		" Virginia	4	F	B				"										
		" Cornelius	1	M	B				"										
12	12	Daily Light	25	M	B				"					/	/				
		" Selena	28	F	B			100	"					/	/				
		" Edward	4	M	B				"										
13	13	Ford Edward	39	M	B	Farmer		150	"					/	/				
		" Susan	36	F	B	HH			"					/	/				
		" Jim	8	M	B				"										
		" Mentor	5	F	B				"										
14	14	Blackwell Abram	23	M	B	Farmer			"					/	/				
		" Fanny	21	F	B	HH			"					/	/				
		" Eddie	3	M	B				"										
		" Bell	1	F	B				"										
		" Lizzie	18	F	B				"						/				
15	15	Fitch Tomy	42	M	B	Farmer		150	"					/	/				
		" Margret	43	F	B	HH			"					/	/				
		" Albert	4	M	B				"										
		" Ann	1	F	B				"										
16	16	Harris Joseph	70	M	M	Farmer	3800	750	Va							/			
		" Milly	45	F	M	HH			Va					/	/				
		" Martha	25	F	M				Tenn										
		" Mary	21	F	M				"										
17	17	Daniel Geo	22	M	M	HH			"						/				
18	18	Ford Robt	23	M	M	Farmer			"					/	/		/		
19	19	Harris James	45	M	M				"					/	/		/		
		" Oley	75	F	B	HH			"					/	/				
		" Chattie	14	M	B				"					/	/				
		" John	13	M	B				"					/	/				
		" Fanny	8	F	B				"										
20	20	Henderson Ned	50	M	B				"										
		" Lilly	37	F	B	HH			"					/	/				
		" Charles	14	M	M				"					/	/				
		" Tom	14	M	M				"					/	/				
		" Henry	12	M	B				"					/	/				

No. of dwellings, 9. No. of white females, ___. No. of males, foreign born, ___.
" families, 9. " colored males, 24. " females, ___.
" white males, ___. " females, 18. " idiot, ___.

The 1870 Census

The Joseph "FreeJoe" Harris family as shown in the United States Census.

148

STATE OF TENNESSEE
STATE BOARD OF HEALTH
Bureau of Vital Statistics
CERTIFICATE OF DEATH

Registration District No. 42407
Primary Registration District No.
File No. 3
Registered No.
(If death occurred in a hospital or institution give its NAME instead of street and number.)

1 PLACE OF DEATH
County Fayette
Civil Dist. #7
or Village Arlington
City

; St.; Ward)

2 FULL NAME Susan Moore

PERSONAL AND STATISTICAL PARTICULARS

3 SEX Female
4 COLOR OR RACE Black
5 SINGLE, MARRIED, WIDOWED, OR DIVORCED (write the word) Widow

6 DATE OF BIRTH (Month) (Day) (Year)

7 AGE About 90 yrs. mos. ds.
If LESS than 1 day......hrs. or......min.?

8 OCCUPATION
(a) Trade, profession, or particular kind of work Domestic
(b) General nature of industry, business, or establishment in which employed (or employer)

9 BIRTHPLACE (State or country) Don't know

10 NAME OF FATHER Joseph Harris
11 BIRTHPLACE OF FATHER (State or country) Robt Harris

12 MAIDEN NAME OF MOTHER "
13 BIRTHPLACE OF MOTHER (State or country) "

PARENTS

14 THE ABOVE IS TRUE TO THE BEST OF MY KNOWLEDGE
(Informant) Arlington Tenn
(Address) Jan 26, 1916

Filed Jan 26, 1916 J. D. Story Registrar

Form V. S. No. 1—2M.

MEDICAL CERTIFICATE OF DEATH

10 DATE OF DEATH January 26th, 1916
(Month) (Day) (Year)

17 I HEREBY CERTIFY, That I attended deceased from
Jan 4, 1914, to Jan 4, 1916,
that I last saw her alive on Jan 4, 1916,
and that death occurred, on the date stated above, at m.

The CAUSE OF DEATH* was as follows:
Senility

Contributory (secondary)

(Duration)... yrs. ...mos. ...ds.

(Duration)... yrs. ...mos. ...ds.

(Signed) E. W. McClanathy M. D.
Jan 26, 1916 (Address) Eads

*State the DISEASE CAUSING DEATH, or, in deaths from VIOLENT CAUSES, state (1) MEANS OF INJURY; and (2) whether ACCIDENTAL, SUICIDAL, or HOMICIDAL.

18 LENGTH OF RESIDENCE (FOR HOSPITALS, INSTITUTIONS, TRANSIENTS, OR RECENT RESIDENTS)
At place of death... yrs. ...mos. ...ds. In the State... yrs. ...mos. ...ds.
Where was disease contracted, if not at place of death?
Former or usual residence.

19 PLACE OF BURIAL OR REMOVAL
DATE OF BURIAL Jan 27, 1916
ADDRESS

20 UNDERTAKER

Death Certificate of Susan "Sucky" Harris-Moore, wife of Simpson Moore, daughter of Joseph "FreeJoe" and Fanny Harris

Note: At the time of her death she was living in the household of Robert and Ella Hamilton, her niece.

149

CERTIFIED COPY OF RECORD OF DEATH.

2161

STATE OF MICHIGAN, } ss.

COUNTY OF Kalamazoo

I, James O. Youngs Clerk of the County of Kalamazoo and of the Circuit Court thereof,

the same being a Court of Record having a seal, do hereby certify that the following is a copy of the record of death of Cornelius H. Harris

now remaining in my office, and of the whole thereof, viz:

RECORD NUMBER	DATE OF DEATH			FULL NAME OF THE DECEASED	MALE OR FEMALE	WHITE, BLACK, MULATTO, ETC.	MARRIED, SINGLE, WIDOW OR WIDOWER	AGE			PLACE OF DEATH
	MONTH	DAY	YEAR					YEARS	MONTHS	DAYS	
10333	February	16	1907	Harris, Cornelius H.	Male	Black	Married?	70	11	13	Oshtemo

DISEASE OR CAUSE OF DEATH	BIRTHPLACE	OCCUPATION	PARENTS		DATE OF RECORD
			NAMES	BIRTHPLACE	
heart trouble	Tenn.	farmer	Joseph Harris	Tenn.	March 7, 1907
			unknown	unknown	

In Testimony Whereof, I have hereunto set my hand and affixed the seal of the Circuit Court, the 24th day of July A.D. 19 95.

JAMES O. YOUNGS Kalamazoo County CLERK.

By DEPUTY CLERK.

Death Certificate of Cornelius H. Harris husband of Emma Minerva Jones-Harris, son of Joseph "FreeJoe" and Fanny Harris

STATE OF TENNESSEE
STATE BOARD OF HEALTH
Bureau of Vital Statistics
CERTIFICATE OF DEATH

Registration District No. _____
Primary Registration District No. _____
Registered No. 315

1 PLACE OF DEATH
County Shelby
Civil Dist.
or Village Grauburg
or City

(If death occurred in a hospital or Institution, give its NAME instead of street and number.)

No. _____ St.; _____ Ward.

2 FULL NAME William M. Harris

PERSONAL AND STATISTICAL PARTICULARS

3 SEX Male 4 COLOR OR RACE Colored 5 SINGLE, MARRIED, WIDOWED, OR DIVORCED (Write the word) Married

6 DATE OF BIRTH 1849 15 Nov (Month) (Day) (Year)

7 AGE 69 yrs. 1 mos. 10 dts. If LESS than 1 day, ____ hrs. or ____ min.?

8 OCCUPATION (a) Trade, profession, or particular kind of work. Farming
(b) General nature of industry, business, or establishment in which employed (or employer).

9 BIRTHPLACE (State or country) Shelby Co.

PARENTS

10 NAME OF FATHER Peter Harris
11 BIRTHPLACE OF FATHER (State or country) Tenn.
12 MAIDEN NAME OF MOTHER Lora Harris
13 BIRTHPLACE OF MOTHER (State or country) Tenn.

14 THE ABOVE IS TRUE TO THE BEST OF MY KNOWLEDGE
(Informant) Will Redman Harris
(Address) Arlington Tenn.

15 Filed Dec 26, 1918. S. B. Webb Registrar.

MEDICAL CERTIFICATE OF DEATH

10 DATE OF DEATH Dec 25, 1918 (Month) (Day) (Year)

17 I HEREBY CERTIFY, That I attended deceased from Dec 10, 1918, to Dec 25, 1918,
that I last saw him alive on Dec 24, 1918,
and that death occurred, on the date stated above, at 9:9 m.

The CAUSE OF DEATH was as follows:
Chronic Brights Disease (Duration) _____ yrs. _____ mos. _____ ds.
Contributory Rockled Kidneys 26 ds.
(secondary)

(Signed) E. L. Sweatte M.D.
Dec 25, 1918. (Address) Collierville

*State the DISEASE CAUSING DEATH, or, in deaths from VIOLENT CAUSES, state (1) MEANS OF INJURY; and (2) whether ACCIDENTAL, SUICIDAL, or HOMICIDAL.

18 LENGTH OF RESIDENCE (FOR HOSPITALS, INSTITUTIONS, TRANSIENTS, OR RECENT RESIDENTS) At place of death ____ yrs. ____ mos. ____ ds. In the State ____ yrs. ____ mos. ____ ds.
Where was disease contracted, if not at place of death?
Former or usual residence.

19 PLACE OF BURIAL OR REMOVAL Mt Morgan DATE OF BURIAL Dec 25, 1918
20 UNDERTAKER S. B. Webb ADDRESS Arlington

Death Certificate of William Harris husband of Nannie Branch-Harris, son of Peter and Laura Ann Jones-Harris, grandson of Joseph "FreeJoe" and Fanny Harris

Note: William's parents were born in Goochland County, Virginia.

151

STATE OF TENNESSEE
STATE DEPARTMENT OF HEALTH
Division of Vital Statistics
CERTIFICATE OF DEATH

File No.
Reg. No. 25234

1. PLACE OF DEATH

County Hardeman.
Civil Dis. #1,
Village Bolivar, Tennessee.

Registration District No.
Primary Registration District No.
(No. Western State Hospital .... St., 2ⁿ Ward)

Ward, Eds., Tenn.

Length of residence in city or town where death occurred 0 yrs. 0 mos. 9 ds.

2. FULL NAME Henry Anderson

(a) Residence: No. RFD 1. Box 138

PERSONAL AND STATISTICAL PARTICULARS

3. SEX — Male
4. COLOR OR RACE — Colored
5. SINGLE, MARRIED, WIDOWED, OR DIVORCED — Married
5a. If married, widowed, or divorced HUSBAND of (or) WIFE of — Louella Anderson
6. DATE OF BIRTH (month, day, and year) — 1851
7. AGE — Years 83
8. Trade, profession, or particular kind of work done, as spinner, lawyer, bookkeeper, etc. — Farmer
9. Industry or business in which work was done, as silk mill, saw mill, bank, etc.
10. Date deceased last worked at this occupation (month and year)
11. Total time (years) spent in this occupation
12. BIRTHPLACE (city or town) (State or country) — Tennessee
13. NAME — Dk.
14. BIRTHPLACE (city or town) (State or country) — Dk.
15. MAIDEN NAME — Dk.
16. BIRTHPLACE (city or town) (State or country) — Dk.
17. INFORMANT — C. S. Anderson (son) (Address) — RFD 1, Box 138, Eds., Tenn.
18. BURIAL, CREMATION, OR REMOVAL — Place Memphis, Tenn. Date
19. UNDERTAKER — M. E. Anderson & Son. (Address) — 2134 Chelsea Ave. Memphis, Tenn.
20. FILED 11-12 — 1934 [signed]

MEDICAL CERTIFICATE OF DEATH

21. DATE OF DEATH (month, day, and year) — 11-4-34
22. I HEREBY CERTIFY, That I attended deceased from 10-26-34 to 11-4-34, that I last saw h. alive on 11-4-34, death is said to have occurred on the date stated above, at 1:30 P.M.

The principal cause of death and related causes of importance in order of onset were as follows:

Contributory causes of importance not related to principal cause

Name of operation
Date of
What test confirmed diagnosis?
Was there an autopsy?

23. If death was due to external causes (violence) fill in also the following:
Accident, suicide, or homicide?
Date of injury
Where did injury occur?
Specify (1) city or town, county, and State) (2) whether injury occurred in industry, in home, or in public place.
Manner of injury
Nature of injury
24. Was disease or injury in any way related to occupation of deceased?

(Signed) [signature] M.D.
(Address)

Date of death 19
death in said

Death Certificate of Henry Anderson, husband of Luella Harris-Anderson

Note: Henry died in Hardeman County, Tennessee.

152

Peter Harris is the son of James "Jim" Harris the grand son of Joseph "Free Joe" and Fanny Harris.

STATE OF TENNESSEE 10394
STATE BOARD OF HEALTH
Bureau of Vital Statistics
CERTIFICATE OF DEATH

Registration District No. 42407
Primary Registration District No.
Registered No. 3

File No.

PLACE OF DEATH
County Fayette
Civil Dist. #1
Village Eads Drive
or City

(If death occurred in a hospital or institution, give its NAME instead of street and number.)

St.; Ward

PERSONAL AND STATISTICAL PARTICULARS

2 FULL NAME Peter Harris

3 SEX M   4 COLOR OR RACE col   5 SINGLE, MARRIED, WIDOWED, OR DIVORCED (Write the word) Married

6 DATE OF BIRTH Apr 1 1847
(Month) (Day) (Year)

7 AGE 87 yrs.   If LESS than 1 day, ... hrs. ... min.

8 OCCUPATION Farmer

9 BIRTHPLACE (State or country) Shelby Co.

PARENTS

10 NAME OF FATHER Jimmy Harris
11 BIRTHPLACE OF FATHER (State or country) Dont know
12 MAIDEN NAME OF MOTHER Alice Leake
13 BIRTHPLACE OF MOTHER (State or country) Dont know

THE ABOVE IS TRUE TO THE BEST OF MY KNOWLEDGE
[Informant] D. J. Harris
[Address] Eads Drive

Filed May 30 1934 Mrs. F. A. Shutten REGISTRAR

MEDICAL CERTIFICATE OF DEATH

16 DATE OF DEATH May 16 1934
(Month) (Day) (Year)

17 I HEREBY CERTIFY, That I attended deceased from May 14 1934 to May 16 1934
that I last saw h... alive on May 16 1934
and that death occurred, on the date stated above, at 10.00 ... M

The CAUSE OF DEATH was as follows:
Nephritis and arterio sclerosis
[Duration] yrs. mos. 3 ds.

Contributory (Secondary) Senile
[Duration] yrs. mos. ds.

Signed R. E. Leaving M. D.
May 17 1934 Address Arlington Tenn.

18 LENGTH OF RESIDENCE (FOR HOSPITALS, INSTITUTIONS, TRANSIENTS, OR RECENT RESIDENTS)
At place of death ... yrs. ... mos. ... ds.   In the State ... yrs. ... mos. ... ds.
Where was disease contracted, if not at place of death?
Former or usual residence

19 PLACE OF BURIAL OR REMOVAL Grassy Creek   DATE OF BURIAL May 18 1934

20 UNDERTAKER A. Wilson & Co   ADDRESS Whitney Gitta

N. B.—Every item of information should be carefully supplied. AGE should be stated EXACTLY. PHYSICIANS should state CAUSE OF DEATH in plain terms, so that it may be properly classified. Exact statement of OCCUPA- TION is very important. See instructions on back of certificate.

MARGIN RESERVED FOR BINDING
WRITE PLAINLY, WITH UNFADING INK—THIS IS A PERMANENT RECORD.

Form V. S. No. 1 1904.   Tennessee Industrial School Print.

Death Certificate of Peter Harris, son of James "Jimmy" Harris, grandson of Joseph "FreeJoe" and Fanny Harris

153

CERTIFICATE OF DEATH

DEPT. OF PUBLIC HEALTH — STATE OF TENNESSEE — DIV. OF VITAL STATISTICS
COOPERATING WITH DEPT. OF COMMERCE — BUREAU OF THE CENSUS

REG. NO. 440
REG. DIST. NO.

73~/

FULL NAME: LUELLA (first) ____ (middle) ANDERSON (last)

2. DATE OF DEATH: JULY 24, 1943 (month, day, year)

3. PLACE OF DEATH:
A) COUNTY: Shelby
B) CITY OR TOWN: Eads, Rural (IF OUTSIDE CITY LIMITS, WRITE RURAL) CIVIL DISTRICT
C) NAME OF HOSPITAL (IF NOT IN HOSPITAL OR INSTITUTION, GIVE STREET ADDRESS)
D) LENGTH OF STAY: IN HOSPITAL ____ IN COMMUNITY 83 Yrs

4. LEGAL RESIDENCE:
A) STATE: Tenn.
B) COUNTY: Shelby CIVIL DISTRICT
C) CITY OR TOWN: Eads, R#1 (IF OUTSIDE CITY LIMITS, GIVE R.F.D. NO.)
D) STREET NO ____
E) CITIZEN OF FOREIGN COUNTRY ____ (YES OR NO)
IF YES, NAME COUNTRY ____

5. RACE OR COLOR: Col.
6. SEX: F
7. SINGLE, MARRIED, WIDOWED, DIVORCED: Widowed
8. AGE: YEARS 83 MONTHS ____ DAYS ____ IF LESS THAN ONE DAY HRS. ____ MINS. ____
9. DATE OF BIRTH: MONTH ____ DAY ____ YEAR ____
10. PLACE OF BIRTH: CITY OR COUNTY Shelby STATE OR COUNTRY Tenn.
11. HUSBAND OR WIFE OF ____
AGE OF HUSBAND OR WIFE, IF LIVING ____ YEARS
12. IF VETERAN NAME OF WAR ____
SOCIAL SECURITY NUMBER ____
13. USUAL OCCUPATION: Housework
14. INDUSTRY OR BUSINESS ____
15. FULL NAME [FATHER]: Porter Harris
BIRTHPLACE: CITY OR COUNTY Shelby STATE OR COUNTRY Tenn.
16. MAIDEN NAME [MOTHER]: Louis Ann Jones
BIRTHPLACE: CITY OR COUNTY Shelby STATE OR COUNTRY Tenn.
17. INFORMANT: John Harris
ADDRESS: Eads, R#1, Bx 150
18. BURIAL, REMOVAL OR CREMATION: DATE July 29, 19 43 PLACE Eads, Tenn.
CEMETERY ____
19. UNDERTAKER: H.C. Jeit
ADDRESS: Collierville

DATE FILED: 7-27- 19 43
BY ____ REGISTRAR

MEDICAL CERTIFICATION

20. I HEREBY CERTIFY THAT I ATTENDED THE DECEASED FROM 7-23- 19 43 TO 7-24- 19 43
AND THAT I LAST SAW H er ALIVE ON 7-23- 19 43
AND THAT DEATH OCCURRED ON THE DATE STATED AT 9 A.M.

IMMEDIATE CAUSE OF DEATH: Cerebral Hemorrhage.   DURATION 2 days.

DUE TO: ____

OTHER CONDITIONS:
(INCLUDE PREGNANCY WITHIN 3 MONTHS OF DEATH)
Acute gastritis from history abt 6 mos.

OPERATION? ____ FINDINGS ____
AUTOPSY? ____ FINDINGS ____

PHYSICIAN UNDERLINE CAUSE TO WHICH DEATH SHOULD BE CHARGED STATISTICALLY

21. IF DEATH WAS DUE TO EXTERNAL CAUSES, FILL IN THE FOLLOWING:
A) ACCIDENT, SUICIDE OR HOMICIDE (SPECIFY) ____
B) DATE OF OCCURRENCE ____
C) WHERE DID INJURY OCCUR ____ CITY ____ COUNTY ____ STATE ____
D) DID INJURY OCCUR IN OR ABOUT HOME, ON FARM, IN INDUSTRIAL PLACE, IN PUBLIC PLACE? ____
WHILE AT WORK ____ MEANS OF INJURY ____

SIGNATURE: W.T. Horton M.D.
ADDRESS ____ DATE SIGNED ____

Death Certificate of Luella Harris-Anderson, wife of Henry Anderson, daughter of Peter and Laura Ann Jones-Harris, granddaughter of Joseph "FreeJoe" and Fanny Harris

Note: Luella's parents were born in Goochland County, Virginia.

154

CERTIFICATE OF DEATH
STATE OF TENNESSEE
DEPT. OF PUBLIC HEALTH
DIVISION OF VITAL STATISTICS

STATE FILE NUMBER

REG. NO. 654
REG. DIST. NO. 802
PRIM. REG.
DIST. NO.

To be inserted by Registrar

If war veteran, give war and military organization.

PLACE OF DEATH:
Shelby

Cordova

Residence in city or town where death occurred _____ yrs. _____ mos. _____ days

(If death occurred in a hospital or institution, give NAME, not street and number)

NAME: ROBERT L. FORD

Cordova, Tenn. RFD#___
(Usual place of abode—If non-resident of place of death, give town and State)

PERSONAL AND STATISTICAL PARTICULARS

4. RACE OR COLOR: Black   5. SINGLE, MARRIED, WIDOWED OR DIVORCED (write the word): Married

BIRTH month _____ day _____ year _____   IF LESS THAN ONE DAY _____ hrs. _____ mins.

AGE: 93 yrs. _____ mos. _____ days

8. TRADE, PROFESSION, OR PARTICULAR KIND OF WORK DONE, AS SPINNER, SAWYER, BOOKKEEPER, ETC.: Retired Farmer.

9. INDUSTRY OR BUSINESS IN WHICH WORK WAS DONE, AS SILK MILL, SAW MILL, BANK, ETC.

10. DATE DECEASED LAST WORKED AT THIS OCCUPATION (month and year): 1915 ?   11. TOTAL TIME (YEARS) SPENT IN THIS OCCUPATION

BIRTHPLACE (city or town): Virginia
(State or country)

13. NAME: Doyle Ford

14. BIRTHPLACE (city or town): (Africa ?)
(State or country)

15. MAIDEN NAME: Charity ------
16. BIRTHPLACE (city or town): Unknown
(State or country)

INFORMANT: Sarah Ford
Cordova, Tenn. (Signature)

BURIAL, CREMATION OR REMOVAL   DATE 12-12-1939

PLACE: Mt. Pisgah

UNDERTAKER: Unite Burial Funeral Home
(Firm name)
Cordova, Tenn.   BY

FILED 12-11-1939   Registrar

MEDICAL CERTIFICATE OF DEATH

21. DATE OF DEATH: Dec. 9 1939
month   day   year

22. I HEREBY CERTIFY, THAT I ATTENDED THE DECEASED FROM July 1938 to Dec. 9, 1939.

I LAST SAW H IM ALIVE ON Sept. 1939 DEATH IS SAID

TO HAVE OCCURRED ON DATE STATED ABOVE, AT 12:40 P M.

THE PRINCIPAL CAUSE OF DEATH AND RELATED CAUSES IN ORDER OF ONSET WERE:

Cerebral Hemorrhage   DATE OF ONSET 12-7-1939

Arteriosclerosis.   ?

CONTRIBUTORY CAUSES OF IMPORTANCE
Senility

NAME OF OPERATION   DATE

WHAT LAB. TEST CONFIRMED DIAGNOSIS?   AUTOPSY? No.

23. IF DEATH WAS DUE TO EXTERNAL CAUSES (VIOLENCE) GIVE FOLLOWING DATA:
ACCIDENT, SUICIDE OR HOMICIDE?   DATE OF INJURY
WHERE DID INJURY OCCUR?
(Specify city or town, county and State)
SPECIFY WHETHER INJURY OCCURRED IN INDUSTRY, IN HOME, OR IN PUBLIC PLACE.
MANNER OF INJURY.
NATURE OF INJURY

24. WAS DISEASE OR INJURY IN ANY WAY RELATED TO OCCUPATION?
IF SO, SPECIFY

(SIGNED) John T. Carter, Jr. M. D.

(ADDRESS)

Death Certificate of Robert Ford, husband of Mary Harris-Ford, son-in-law of Joseph "FreeJoe" and Fanny Harris

155

CERTIFICATE OF DEATH

STATE OF MICHIGAN ⎱ ss.
County of Kent ⎰

I, TERRI L. LAND, ▬▬▬▬▬▬▬▬▬▬▬▬ Clerk of the Circuit Court

for said County of Kent, do hereby certify that upon careful examination of the original records on file in

the office of the Clerk of said County and Court, I find the following records as to the death of

EMMA HARRIS

Date of Death.................... JULY 8, 1929

Full Name of Deceased.................... EMMA HARRIS

Sex....Female....Color....White........Marital Status: Widow

Age....82....Years....11....Months....2....Days

Place of Death.................... Grand Rapids, Michigan

Disease or Cause of Death.................... Cancer of the Bladder

Birthplace.................... Tennessee

Occupation.................... Retired

Name of Father.................... Thomas Jones....Virginia

Name of Mother.................... Adeline Childs....North Carolina

All of which appears as of record dated.................... July 31, 1929

and the same being the whole of such original record of the death of said deceased, as

Recorded in Liber....14....of RECORD OF DEATHS, at page....76

IN TESTIMONY WHEREOF, I have hereunto set my hand

and official seal, at the City of Grand Rapids, in said County,

this....8th....day of....January....A. D. 19..96

TERRI L. LAND, Clerk

.... Deputy

D-1

Death Certificate of Emma Minerva Jones-Harris, daughter of Jefferson M. and Adeline "Lettie" Harris-Jones, wife of Cornelius H. Harris, granddaughter and daughter-in-law of Joseph "FreeJoe" and Fanny Harris
Note: Cornelius and Emma were uncle and niece.

PRESS # No 0229

CERTIFICATE OF DEATH

MICHIGAN DEPARTMENT OF PUBLIC HEALTH
Office of the State Registrar
and Center for Health Statistics

State Office No.
2-35

Registered No. 61

PLACE OF DEATH

County Kalamazoo
Township
Village
City Kalamazoo (No. _____ St. _____ Ward)
(If death occurred in a hospital or institution, give its NAME instead of street and number.)

FULL NAME Virginia Phillips

SEX	COLOR OR RACE	MARITAL STATUS	AGE:	YEARS	MONTHS	DAYS	BIRTHPLACE
Female	Malotto	Married	46	46	01	05	Tennessee

OCCUPATION OF DECEASED Housekeeper

DATE OF DEATH June 5, 18 1878

CAUSE OF DEATH Consumption

NAME OF FATHER Joseph Harris

RESIDENCE OF FATHER Kalamazoo

NAME OF MOTHER Fannie Harris

RESIDENCE OF MOTHER Kalamazoo

I hereby certify that the above is a true and correct transcript of the record of death on file in the Michigan Department of Public Health.

Filed 09-01- 18 79

George Jean Cully
State Registrar

T. Ludwig
Registrar

Lansing, Michigan

November 9, 1993

B37b 5/92

Death Certificate of Virginia Harris-Phillips, wife of Wesley Phillips, daughter of Joseph "FreeJoe" and Fanny Harris

Note: Virginia's parents were born in Goochland County, Virginia and they resided in Eads, Tennessee.

157

STATE OF TENNESSEE, SHELBY COUNTY.

MARRIAGE LICENSE.

To any one Legally Authorized to Solemnize Marriages:

These are to Authorize you to *solemnize the rites of Matrimony between*

Davie Green and *Roda Guy*

of your County, agreeably to an Act of the General Assembly, in such case made and provided; provided that there is no lawful cause to obstruct the marriage for which this License is desired; otherwise these shall be null and void, and shall not be accounted any license or authority for you, or either of you, for the purpose aforesaid, more than if the same had never been prayed or granted.

Given under my hand, at the Clerk's Office, in said County, this 30th day of *January* 1869

_____ CLERK.

By_____ D. C.

CERTIFICATE.

STATE OF TENNESSEE, }
SHELBY COUNTY.

I SOLEMNIZED THE RITE OF MATRIMONY *between the within named parties,*

on the 20a day of *Feby* 1869

Sen Monroe, Past.

Returned on the 1st day of *March* 1869

_____ CLERK.

By R. Cole _____ D. C.

Marriage License of Davie Green and Roda (Rhoda) Harris-Guy, daughter of Joseph "FreeJoe" and Fanny Harris

158

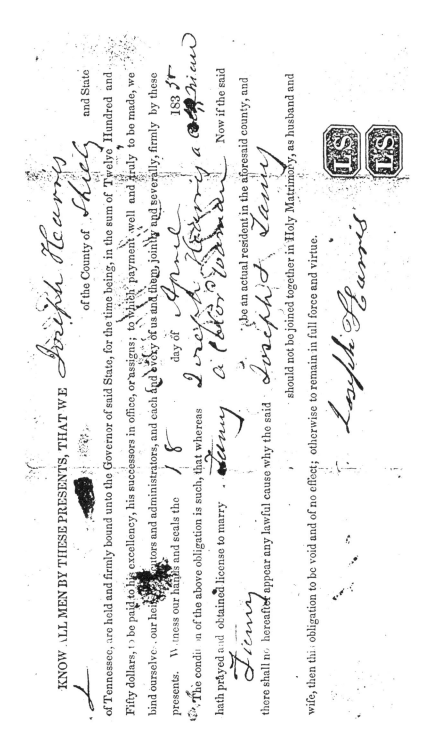

Marriage License of Joseph and Fanny

On April 18, 1835, Joseph and Fanny Harris became the first African-American couple to marry in Shelby County, Tennessee.

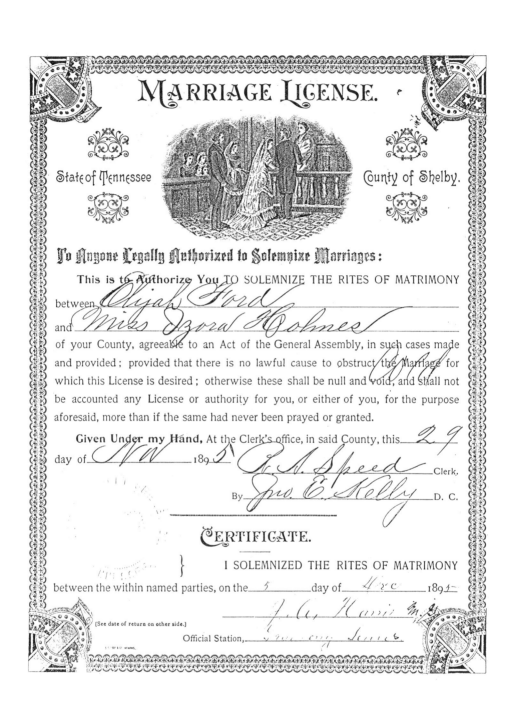

MARRIAGE LICENSE.

State of Tennessee   County of Shelby.

To Anyone Legally Authorized to Solemnize Marriages:

This is to Authorize You TO SOLEMNIZE THE RITES OF MATRIMONY between *Elijah Ford* and *Miss Izora Holmes* of your County, agreeable to an Act of the General Assembly, in such cases made and provided; provided that there is no lawful cause to obstruct the Marriage for which this License is desired; otherwise these shall be null and void, and shall not be accounted any License or authority for you, or either of you, for the purpose aforesaid, more than if the same had never been prayed or granted.

Given Under my Hand, At the Clerk's office, in said County, this *29* day of *Nov* 189*5*   *E. A. Speed* Clerk.

By *Jno. E. Kelly* D. C.

CERTIFICATE.

}   I SOLEMNIZED THE RITES OF MATRIMONY between the within named parties, on the *5* day of *Dec* 189*5*

J. C. Harris M.

[See date of return on other side.]

Official Station, *_____*

Marriage License of Elijah Ford and Izora Holmes, son of Robert and Mary Harris-Ford, grandson of Joseph "FreeJoe" and Fanny Harris

160

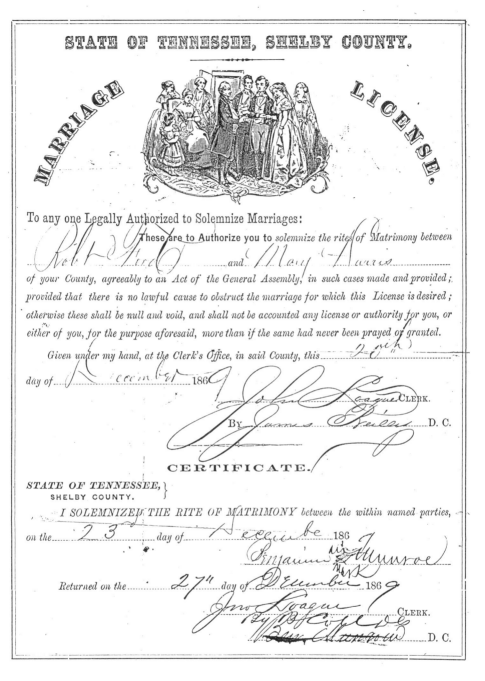

STATE OF TENNESSEE, SHELBY COUNTY.

MARRIAGE LICENSE.

To any one Legally Authorized to Solemnize Marriages:

These are to Authorize you to *solemnize the rites of Matrimony between* _Robt Ford_ and _Mary Harris_ *of your County, agreeably to an Act of the General Assembly, in such cases made and provided; provided that there is no lawful cause to obstruct the marriage for which this License is desired; otherwise these shall be null and void, and shall not be accounted any license or authority for you, or either of you, for the purpose aforesaid, more than if the same had never been prayed or granted.*

Given under my hand, at the Clerk's Office, in said County, this _20th_ *day of* _December_ 186_9_

John Loague CLERK.

By _James Skillen_ D. C.

CERTIFICATE.

STATE OF TENNESSEE,
SHELBY COUNTY.

I SOLEMNIZED THE RITE OF MATRIMONY between the within named parties, *on the* _23_ *day of* _December_ 186_9_

Benjamin Munroe

Returned on the _27"_ *day of* _December_ 186_9_

Jno Loague CLERK.

By _B Coyle_ D. C.

Wm Glasgow D. C.

Marriage License of Mary Harris and Robert Ford, daughter of Joseph "FreeJoe" and Fanny Harris

Note: Mary died in an accident seven weeks before her father's death in 1875. Alonzo, Mary's youngest son died in October of 1875 from injuries as a result of the accident.

161

Wesley Phillips
To
Virginia Harris

November 14th 1849, a marriage License issued in the words and figures following to wit:

The State of Indiana } Set.
Jennings County }

To any person legally authorized to Solemnize the rites of matrimony greeting: This is therefore to License and permit you to join together in the holy State of matrimony Wesley Phillips to Virginia Harris, and for so doing this shall be your sufficient warrant.

L.S. In testimony whereof I have hereunto set my hand and seal of office, at Vernon, this 14th day of November 1849.
Wm. P. Shields, Clerk
By Jas. M. Hill Dep.

State of Indiana Jennings County Ss.
This Is to Certify that I did on the 15th of Nov. 1849 join together in the holy State of matrimony Wesley Phillips to Virginia Harris —
Dennis Cagley M.G.

Filed & Recorded 26. Nov. 1849

Marriage License of Wesley and Virginia Harris-Phillips
November 15, 1849
Vernon, Indiana

162

State of Tennessee,

SHELBY COUNTY.   KNOW ALL MEN BY THESE PRESENTS :

That we......

of the County of Shelby and State of Tennessee, are held and firmly bound to the State of Tennessee in the sum of Twelve Hundred and Fifty Dollars, to which payment well and truly to be made, we bind ourselves, our heirs, executors and administrators, and each and every one of us, jointly and severally by these presents.

Witness our hands and seals, this......4th......day of......October......186 9

....[SEAL.]

....[SEAL.]

THE CONDITION OF THE ABOVE OBLIGATION IS SUCH, that, whereas, the above bounden .... has this day prayed and obtained a license to marry... now if there is no lawful cause to obstruct said marriage and for which license is desired, then this obligation to be void, otherwise to remain in full force and virtue in law.

ATTEST:...

.....................................Clerk.

BY.......................................D. C.

Marriage License of Joseph and Millie

On October 4, 1869, Joseph "FreeJoe" Harris and Millie Wash were married. He was 73 years old and she was 45 years old.

163

Where as a marriage is contemplated between the undersign Joseph Harris on the one part and Milly Wash on the other part and the riches of matrimony between these are about to be solemnized – therefore this agreement witnessth............

That for and in consideration of said marriage the said Joseph Harris an his part agrees to make to the said Milly Wash his intended future wife, a deed to thirty acres of land to be taken from the west part or portion of the tract of land on which he now lives..... to give her one horse and two cows and to erect at the expense of his estate after his death a suitable cabin & accompanying out house, on the said land so agrees to be given & deeded to the said Milly Wash should she be the longest liver and survive the said Joseph Harris.

In consideration therefor the said Milly Wash on her part agrees and here does grant claim and abandon all rights, title, claims and interest which by virtue of her marriage and survivorship as his widow she might have and agree under the law in such case made and provide if in lieu of the estate of the said Joseph Harris wish to his widow and distributes accepting the provision she is made in full in lieu of all material rights and okay legation to which she would be entitled in the absence of the agreement and contract.

It is expressly understood and agreed by and between the parties that in the event of the failure of the valorization of the riches of matrimony between the said Joseph Harris and Milly Wash & for any cause, this contract is null and void.

Prenuptial Agreement
On October 1, 1869, Joseph "FreeJoe" Harris and Millie Wash, his bride-to-be entered into a marriage contract.

164

*In testimony whereof we have set our hand & seal
this 1st. day of October A. D. 1869...........*

*Joseph Harris
Milly Wash
(her mark x)*

Prenuptial Agreement (cont.).

Whereas a marriage is contemplated between the undersigned Joseph Harris on the one part and Milly Nash on the other part and the rites of matrimony between them are about to be solemnized — therefore this agreement witnesseth —

That for and in consideration of said marriage the said Joseph Harris on his part agrees to make to the said Milly Nash his intended future wife, a deed to _Thirty acres of land_ to be taken from the west part a portion of the tract of land on which he now lives — To give to her _One Horse_ and _two cows_ and to erect at the expense of his estate after her death a said all necessary out house, on the said land So agrees to be given by deed &c to the said Milly Nash Should she be the longest liver and survive the said Joseph Harris —

In Consideration thereof the said Milly Nash on her part agrees and hereby does quit claim and abandon all right title claim

and interest which by virtue of her
marriage and survivorship as
his widow she might have and a
guard under the laws in such case
made and provided of in and to
the Estate of the said Joseph Harris both as his widow and dis-
tributee accepting the provision
herein made as [...] in lieu
of all marital rights and obligations to which she would be
Entitled in the absence of this a-
greement and Contract —

It is expressly
understood and agreed by and
between the Parties, that in the E-
vent of the failure of the solemn-
ization of the rites of matrimony between the said Joseph Harris and Milly Wash from any
Cause, this Contract is null &
void —

In testimony whereof we
have set our hands & seals, this 1st
Day of October A.D. 1869 —

Signed & acknowledged in Joseph Harris (Seal)
in presence before the mar-
riage of the parties Signing Milly Wash (Seal)
[...] her mark +

W. S. Gray

Prenuptial Agreement (cont.).

167

This indenture made and entered into this tenth day of February one thousand eight
hundred and forty nine between Richard Leake of the first part and Joseph Harris of the
second part all of Shelby county & state of Tennessee witnessth that the said Richard
Leake for and in consideration of the sum of six hundred dollars to have in hand paid
hath this day promised, bargain and sold and conveyed and by these presents doth grant
bargain sell & convey to said Joseph one certain tract or parcel of land lying & being in
the county of Shelby and the state of Tennessee in the eleventh district range four and
section three and bounders as follows beginning at a stake the north east corner of said
section running west fifty poles and fourteen links to a stake with elm dogwood & black
oak pointers thence south: three hundred & seventeen poles & fifteen links to a stake elm
& ash & persimmon pointers thence east forty poles & fourteen links to stake eighteen
links east of a sweet gum marker 766 & which stake is the southeast corner of Tennessee
Cumberland college tract no 23116 thence north three hundred & seventeen poles fifteen
links to the beginning containing by actual survey one hundred acres and the said Richard
Leake doth hereof said himself his heirs executors & assigns to warrant & defend the
title to said land to the said Joseph Harris his heirs executors & assigns from the claim of
any other person or persons whatever from this day forth and forever. In testimony
whereof I here unto subscribe my name & offer my seal this day and date above witnessth
and in the presents of

W.G. Lancaster
S.A. Leake
John Nolels

Richard Leake

Land Purchase

**On February 10, 1849, Joseph purchased 100 acres of land for
the sum total of $600.00 from Richard Leake. Richard Leake was the
brother of Samuel Leake.**

This Indenture made and Entered into this Tenth day of February one thousand Eight hundred and forty nine between Richard Seake of the first part and Joseph Harris of the second part all of Shelby County & State of Tennessee witnesseth that the said Richard Seake for and in consideration of the sum of Six hundred Dollars to him in hand paid hath this day granted bargained & Sold and Conveyed & by these presents doth grant bargain sell & Convey to the said Joseph one certain tract or parcel of land lying & being in the County of Shelby and State of Tennessee in the ninth district range four & section three and described as follows Beginning at a Stake the North East Corner of land ... ... west fif...

... and fourteen links to a stake with Iron Dogwood & black oak pointers thence South three hundred & seventeen poles & fifteen links to a stake Elm Ash & persimmon pointers thence East fifty poles & fourteen links to a stake Eighteen links East of a Sycamore marked J64 & which Stake is the South East corner of Tennessee Cumberland College tract No 9316 thence North three hundred & Seventeen poles fifteen links to the Beginning Containing by actual Survey one hundred Acres and the said Richard Seake doth herself bind himself his heirs Executors & assigns to Warrant & defend the title to said land to the said Joseph Harris his heirs Executors & assigns from the Claim of any other person or persons whatsoever from this day forth and forever In testimony whereof I have to Subscribe my name & affix my seal this day and date above written

Witness the present of
W H Lancaster
J A Seake
John Nails

Richd Seake (Seal)

July 20, 1834

Land Purchase

On July 20, 1834, Joseph "FreeJoe" Harris purchased fifty (50) acres of land from W.T. Royster for $100.00.

This indenture made and entered into this 20th of July in the year of our Lord one thousand eight hundred & thirty four between T.W. Royster of the county of Shelby and state of Tennessee of the first part and Jos Harris of the said county and state aforesaid of the second part witnesspeth that the said party of the first part for and in consideration of the sum of one hundred dollars to me in hand paid by the said party of the second part the rest is truly acknowledged hath granted bargained sold acknowledged and by these presents doth grant bargain sell & convey unto the said party of the second part his heirs and assigns forever a certain tract or parcel of land situated lying & being in county & state aforesaid in the eleventh surveyors district in range 4 & section 3 and being part of the entry in the name of John Lewis no 758 beginning on the west boundary line of a 200 acre occupant in the name of Wilson Wade with a warrant at Samuel Leake coming in the Stage Road south of a white oak marker with a mark thence north along said Wade his no 275 links to a stake a thin post oak pointer thence west 20 chains & 33 links to a black oak with 4 post oak pointers thence south 326 chains 75 links to a stake 1 chain north of a post oak marker J 26 two post oaks of hickory pointers thence south eighty seven & half east along said road 13 chains thence south twenty six east 76 chains 81 links to the being containing fifty acres more or less to have and hold the above described land with its appurtenances to the -----& behoof benefit of the said party of the second part his heirs- administration executing and assigns and further this as the said party of the first part his heirs executor and assigns will warrant and forever defend the right and title to the aforesaid land with its appurtenances unto the said party of the second part his heirs and assigns against all lawful demands of persons in witness whereof I have here unto set my hand and seal this day & date first written. Signed Sealed & Delivered.

T.W. Royster

We Jno B. Lancaster & Lucy Lancaster have this day bargained and sold and do hereby transfer and assign to Joseph Harris and his heirs, forever for the consideration of six hundred and seventy eight dollars and seventy cents to me, baird a tract of same in the state of Tennessee, Shelby County and District Row 829, containing by estimation forty five acres be the same more or less and bounded as follows on the north by the parcel of Ms. Clayten formerly known as the Lamp of Jm Nobles, and on the east by lot No. 1, drawn by M.C Leake and on the south by W.F. Williams and Mrs. Nelly Williams, and on the west by the remaining fifty acres of lot No. 2. To have and to hold the same to the said Jos Harris, his heirs and assigns forever, we do covenant with the said Jos Harris that we are lawfully surrogates of said land, have a good right to carry it and that the same is unincumbered, we do further covenant and bind ourselves our heirs and representatives to warrant and forever defend the title to the said land and every part thereof to the said Jos Harris his heirs and assigns against the lawful claims of all persons whatsoever this the 12th day of Sept 1854.

Jno B. Lancaster
Lucy V. Lancaster

Witness

Wm. G. Lancaster
M.E. Cochran

The following are the corners and pointers of said tract beginning at a stake the N.W. of Lot No. 1 and N.E. corner of Lot No. 2 of the 640 acre tract belonging to the heirs of Rich Leake and running west 6 chains 93 links to a stake 20 links No. 53 1/2 east of a real Oak marked 36 thence & 79 chains 40 links to a stake in Gray's Creek with Red Bud White Oak Dogwood and Spanish Oak pointers thence & 6 chains 93 links to a stake thence north 79 chains 40 links to the beginning Sept 12th 1854.

Jno B. Lancaster
Lucy V. Lancaster

Witness

W. G. Lancaster
M.E. Cochran

Land Purchase

Joseph purchased a 55-acre track of land from J.B. and Lucy Lancaster for the sum total of $678.70. J.B. and Lucy Lancaster were the son-in-law and daughter of Richard Leake.

Continued... Done at office this 23rd day of October AD 1854
John B. Sergeant Clerk

We Jno. B. Lancaster & Lucy V. Lancaster ha... this day
bargained and sold and do hereby transfer and convey to Joseph
Harris and his Heirs, forever, for the Consideration of Six Hundred and Seventy Eight dollars and Seventy Cents to me paid a
tract of Land in the State of Tennessee Shelby County and District
Nos 8 & 9 Containing by estimation Fifty Five Acres be the same
More or less And bounded as follows on the North by the lands
of Mr. Clayton formerly known as the lands of Jno. Nibbs and
on the East by lot No 1 drawn by M. E. Leake and on the South
by H. S. Williams and Mrs. Molly Williams And on the West
by the remaining Fifty Acres of lot No 2. To have and to
Hold the same to the said Jos. Harris his heirs and Assigns
forever. We do Covenant With the said Jos. Harris that we are
lawfully siezed of said lands, have a good Right to convey it
And that the same is unincumbered We do further Covenant
And bind ourselves our Heirs and Representatives to Warrant
And forever defend the Title to the said Land and every
part thereof to the said Jos. Harris, his Heirs And Assigns again
the lawful Claims of all persons Whatsoever This the 18th day
of Septr 1854   Jno. B. Lancaster (Seal)
Witness   Lucy V. Lancaster (Seal)
Wm. S. Lancaster
M. E. Cochran

The following are the Corners and pointers of said tract
Beginning at a stake the N.W. of lot No 1 And the N.E. Corner
of lot No 2 of the 160 acre tract belonging to the heirs of Rich'd Leake
and running West 6 Chains 23 links to a stake 20 links N 55° E of
a red Oak Marked H. thence S 79 Chains 40 links to a stake on
Cave Creek With red bud White Oak Dogwood and Spanish
... for ... thence E ... Chains ... links to a stake the ...

C.A. STARR to
JOSEPH HARRIS

This indenture made and entered into this 25th day of
November in the year of our Lord one thousand eight hundred
and sixty five between C.A. Starr of the one part and Joseph
Harris of the other part, both of county of Shelby and state
of Tennessee witnesspeth that the said C.A. Starr for and in
consideration of the sum of six hundred and eighty dollars
receipt whereof is hereby acknowledged that the said C. A.
Starr has this day bargained and sold and by these presents
conveyed and transfers to the said Joseph Harris and his
heirs forever a certain tract of land in Shelby county,
state of Tennessee and in district NO. 8 & 9 containing by
estimation fifty acres and bounded as follows: beginning at
a stake with a red oak pointer marker II-II on the north
west corner of Joseph Harris' fifty five acre tract bought
of J. B. and Lucy V. Lancaster running west to a stake in
the north east corner of R. W. Leake's lot No. 3 now
belonging to the heirs of Phillip Webber. Thence south 79
chains 40 links to a stake in the south east corner of a
aforemention lot NO. 3 with two maple from lies thence east
to a stake in Gray's Creek on the south west corner of
Joseph Harris' fifty-five acre tract with red bird & white
oak dogwood and spanish oak pointers. Thence north seventy
nine chains 40 links to the beginning. To have and to hold
the same to the said Joseph Harris his heirs and assigns
forever with this reservation, that the said C.A. Starr
claims for himself and heirs forever the right of way for a
road leading to the main Sommerville and Memphis Road, the
said road so be at least twenty feet wide and remain where
it now seems upon said tract of land, or if changed so be
upon same part of said tract of land easily accepible so the
above mentioned.
I do further covenant and agree with the said Joseph Harris
that I am lawfully seized of said land have a good right to
convey it and that the same is unencumbered. I do further
bind my heirs and representatives to warrant and defend to
the said Joseph Harris his heirs and assigns the title to
the said land as an indefeasable inheritance in fee simple
exquish the claims of all persons whatever.

C.A.Starr

Witnesp
Henry T. Bragg
Wm. A. Redd

Land Purchase

**On November 25, 1865, Joseph "FreeJoe" Harris purchased fifty (50)
acres of land for the sum total of $680.00 from C.A. Starr. This land was
a gift to James Harris, one of FreeJoe's sons.**

174

November 25, 1865

This Land was a gift
To James Harris, the
Son of "FreeJoe" Harris

This Indenture Made this 1st day of December of the Year, One Thousand Eight Hundred and fifty Eight between F. H. Talley, of the one part and Joe Harris of the other, both of the County of Shelby, of the State of Tennessee Witnesseth, that the said F. H. Talley, for and in Consideration of the Sum of twelve hundred dollars four hundred of which Sum is paid to said F. H. Talley, in Cash and two hundred by Note of said Joe Harris Dec 28th December 1858 the receipt of which is hereby acknowledged the remaining Six hundred dollars to be paid within (18) eighteen Months from date, has bargained and sold and by these presents do Convey and Confirm to the said Joe Harris his heirs and assigns forever a Certain tract or piece of Land lying in the aforesaid County and State, Containing (by a recent Survey) One Hundred and twelve acres of Land and being a part of the estate of the late Richard Leaker the metes and bounds of which are as follows, vizzy beginning at a Stake in the South line of Mrs Clay's land and in the N W Corner of Joe Harris 100 acre tract thence West 14 Chains 16 links to a stake in the N E Corner of Joe Harris 55 acre tract with red oak and Hickory Pointers, thence South 79 Chains 50 links to a stake on the South side of Grays Creek with Hickory and ash Pointers, thence east 14 Chains 16 links to a Stake in Mrs Williams North line, the South West Corner of Joe Harris 100 acre tract with persimmon and sweet gum Pointers, thence North 79 Chains 50 links to the beginning, which tract of Land together with the hereditaments and appurtenances thereunto belonging to the said F. H. Talley, and the said Joe Harris his heirs and assigns will Warrant and defend forever against the lawful Claims of himself and all persons whomsoever by these presents, as an indefeasible inheritance in fee Simple, In Testimony Whereof the said F. H. Talley has hereunto put his hand and affixed his Seal this the first day of December one thousand Eight Hundred and fifty Eight

F. H. Talley (Seal)
M. C. Talley (Seal)

Signed Sealed and delivered in presence of.

This indenture made this 1st day of December of the year one thousand eight hundred and fifty eight between F.H. Talley, of the one part and Joe Harris of the other both of the county of Shelby of the state of Tennessee. Witnesseth that the said F.H. Talley for and in consideration of the sum of twelve hundred dollars four hundred of which sum is paid to said F.H. Talley in cash two hundred by note of said Joe Harris due 25th December, 1858 the receipt of which is hereby acknowledged the remaining six hundred dollars to be paid within (18) eighteen months from date has bargained and sold and by these presents do convey and confirm to the said Joe Harris, his heirs and assigns forever a certain tract or piece of land lying in the aforesaid county and state containing (by a recent survey) one hundred and twelve acres of land and being a part of the estate of the late Richard Leake the metes and bounds of which are as follows. Beginning at a stake in the south line of Wm. Royster's land and in the NW corner of Joe Harris' 100 acre tract thence west 14 chains, 10 links to a stake in the NE corner of said Joe Harris' 55 acre tract's withered oak and hickory pointers thence south 79 chains, 50 links to a stake in the south line of Grays' Creek north hickory and oak pointers thence east 14 chains 10 links to a stake on Wm. Williams' north line the southwest corner of Joe Harris' 100 acre tract with persimmon and sweet gum pointers thence north 79 chains 50 links to the beginning which said tract of land together with the hereitaments and appurtenances thereunto belonging to the said F.H. Talley unto the said Joe Harris, his heirs and assigns will warrant and defend forever against the lawful claims of himself and all persons whomsoever by these presents as an indefeasible inheritance in fee simple. In testimoney whereof the said F. H. Talley has hereunto put his hand and affixed his seal the the first day of December one thousand eight hundred and fifty eight.

F.H. Talley
M.C. Talley

Land Purchase (cont.)

177

This Indenture, made and entered into this 23 day of December in the year of our Lord One Thousand Eight _red and fifty eight between _e _arris of the County of _____ and State of Tennessee of the first p___ and D. R. R_____ of the said County and State aforesaid of the second part, Witnesseth that the said party of the first part for and in con_____ tion of the sum of $ 250 to be paid in hand the 1st of ____ 1359 by the party of the 2nd part and Two hundred fifty ___ to me in hand June 1860 by the party of the 2nd part is hereby acknowledged hath granted bargained sold and conveyed and by these presents doth grant bargain sell and convey ___ the said party of the second part his heirs and assigns forever certain tract or parcel of Land situated lying and being ___ County and State aforesaid on the Eleventh Surveyors District in Range 4 and Section 3 and being a part of the Entry in the name of the heirs of John _____ c_ 789 Beginning on the West boundary line of a 200 acre Occupant ___ that of Wilson Wade with a Warrant at Samuel Lakes corner the Stage Road South of a White Oak marked with X _____ thence North along said Wades line 26 chains 75 links _ stake and 3 Post Oak pointers, thence West 20 chains __ __ to a Black Oak with four post oak pointers thence South __ chains 75 links to a stake 1 chain North a Post Oak ____ I N two post oaks 1 Hickory pointers, thence South Eight ___ and half E along said Road 13 chains thence South _____ one East 7 chains 11 links to the Beginning, Containing ___ acre more or less to have and to hold the above described ___ with its appurtenances to the only use and behoof and ben___ of the said party of the second part his heirs administra____ heirs and assigns and father he the said party of the first part his heirs, Executors administrators and assigns will Warrant and forever defend the right and title to the aforesaid land with the appurtenances unto the said party of the second part his heirs assigns against all lawful demands of persons.
In Witness Whereof I have hereunto set my hand and Seal the day and date first written
I N 18 May 16 /59   Joseph Harris

December 23,1858

Land Sale

On December 23, 1858 Joseph "FreeJoe" Harris sold fifty (50) acres of land for the sum total of $250.00 to D.R. Royster.

178

This indenture made and entered into the 23rd day of
December in the year of our lord one thousand eight hundred
and fifty eight between Joe Harris of the county of Shelby
and state of Tennessee of the first part and D. R. Royster
of the said county and state aforesaid of the second part,
witnesseth that the said party of the first part for and in
consideration of the sum of $250.00 to be paid in hand the
1st of July 1859 by the party of the 2nd part and two
hundred fifty paid to me in hand give 1860 by the party of
the 2nd part & is hereby acknowledged hath granted bargained
sold and conveyed and by these presents doth grant bargain
sell and convey unto the said party of the second part his
heirs and assigns forever a certain track or parcel of land
situated lying and being in the county and state aforesaid
in the eleventh surveyors district in range 4 and section 3
and being a part of the entry in the name of the heirs of
John Ton No. 789 beginning on the west boundry line of a 200
acre occupant in the name of Wilson Wade with a warrant at
Samuel Leake's corner in the Stage Road south of a white oak
marker with X mark thence south along said Wattes' line 26
chains 75 links to a stake and 3 pot oak pointers, thence
west 20 chains 25 links to a black oak with four post oak
pointers, thence south 22 chains 75 links to a stake 1 chain
north a post oak marker J.H. two post oakes & hickory
pointers, thence south eighty-seven and a half & along said
road 13 chains thence south seventy one east 7 chains 81
links to the beginning, containing fifty acres more or less
to have and to hold the above described land with its
appurtenances to the only use and behoof and benefit of the
said party of the second part his heirs administrations
executors and assigns will warrant and faces defend the
right and title to the aforesaid land with its appurtenances
unto the said party of the second part his heirs assigns
against all lawful demands of persons.

In witness whereof I have herewith set my hand and seal the
day and date first written.

J.H.H. May 16, 1859
Joseph Harris

The Route from Goochland County, Virginia
to Shelby County, Tennessee

This map shows the route that Joseph "FreeJoe" Harris and the plantation owners, Samuel Leake, Richard Leake, the Ellis and Starr families took with their equipment and slaves to Shelby County.

The wagon train began in Goochland County, approximately 40-45 miles west of Richmond, Virginia on the Great Indian Warpath trail. They traveled through Lynchburg and Roanoke, Virginia to Bristol, Virginia to Tennessee. They continued on to Morristown and Knoxville, Tennessee, across the Tennessee River in a westward direction on the Cumberland Trace to Nashville, Tennessee. In Nashville they took the lower Harpeth trail which ran into the Chickasaw trail and on to the Bolivar and Memphis trail which brought them into Shelby County, Tennessee.

Many of the trails used by the early settlers were formed initially by animals and developed by native Americans and early settlers. Many of yesterday's trails are now today's highways and interstates.

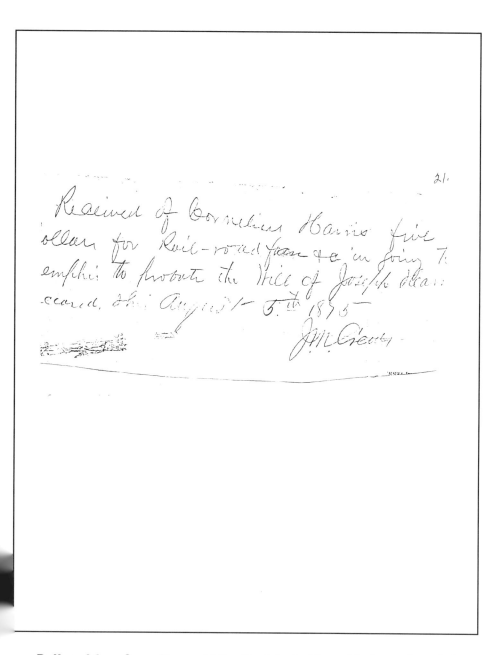

21.

Received of Cornelius Harris five
dollars for Rail-road fare &c in going to
emphis to probate the Will of Joseph dec-
ceased, this August 5th 1895 —

J.M. Green

Railroad fare Cornelius paid for the trip to Memphis to probated the will of Joseph "FreeJoe" Harris.

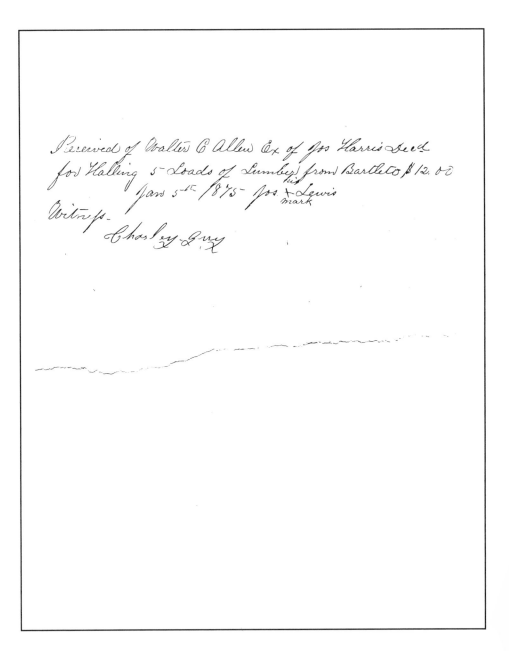

Received of Walter C Allen Ex of Jos Harris deed
for Halling 5 Loads of Lumber from Bartleto $12.00
                    Jan 5th 1875 Jos + Lewis
                                       his
                                       mark
Witness-
        Charley Guy

**Pay received from the Joseph "FreeJoe" Harris estate
for services rendered.**

182

1875.   Jos. Harris Dr To Rhoda Green
To hire of Ella Guy 7 months.
commencing the 1st day of Jan/1875
and worked until the last of July 1875 - $15.00
    Cr by Cash   6.00
    Ballance due $9.00

Sworn to and subscribed before
me January 7st 1876   Rhoda + Green
                         her mark

Rhoda Green received pay that was due Ella Guy, who was deceased, from the estate of Joseph "FreeJoe" Harris.

183

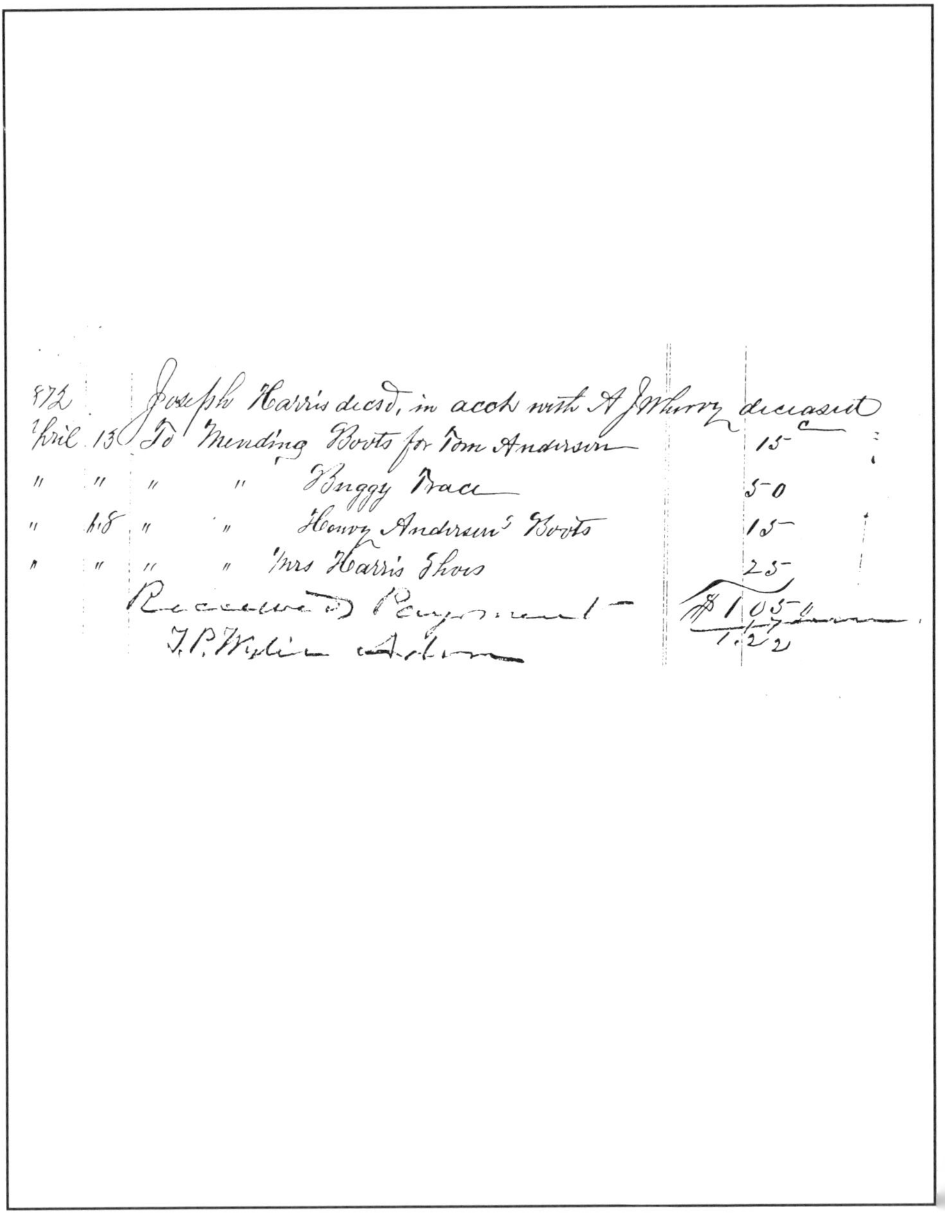

872

Joseph Harris dicsd, in acct with A J Wherry dicasd

April 13 To Mending Boots for Tom Anderson — 15

"   "   "   " Buggy Trace — 5-0

"   18 "   " Henry Anderson' Boots 15

"   "   "   " Mrs Harris Shoes 25

Received Payment — $1 05

J. P. Wylie Adm 1 2 2

Shoe repair paid by the estate of Joseph "FreeJoe" Harris to the estate of A.J. Wherry.

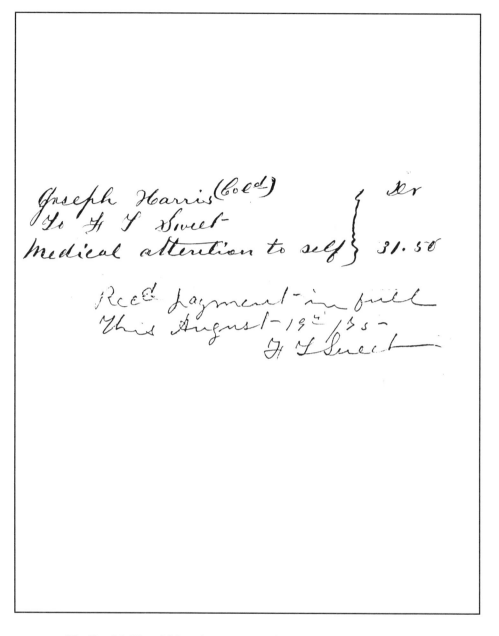

Medical bill paid by the estate of Joseph "FreeJoe" Harris.

August th 6th 1875

This is to certify that we the under signed heirs of Jos. Harris deceased. do hereby ortherise Mr Walter Allen Ex of the Estate of said Jos. Harris deseased to pay to Brother Cornelius Harris out of any money or monies that may be in his possession belonging to the said Estate of Joseph Harris deceased. this shall be of the undevided means on hand. the ammount as follow

Rail Road fair	$ 48.50	forty Eight dollars fifty cts
Witness dinner	1.50	one dollar fifty cts
for horses at Bartlet	50	fifty cts
To Col. Crews	$ 5.00	five dollars
	$ 55.60	Amount fifty five dollars fifty

Rose Iche
Martha Branch
Robert his + mark Trask
Cornelius Harris.

The heirs of Joseph "FreeJoe" Harris advise the estate to pay the traveling expenses of Cornelius Harris for his trip from Kalamazoo, Michigan.

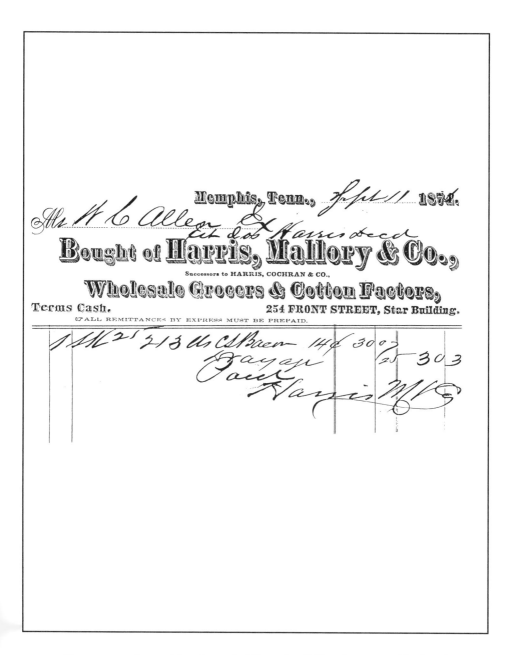

Bacon purchased by Joseph "FreeJoe" Harris on credit for the Inn was paid by the estate.

Bartlett, Tenn., *Sept 11* 1875 2

Mrs. A. C. Allen for Estate of Jos. Harris Decd

Bought of **WRIGHT, SHELBY & SHOTWELL,**

DEALERS IN

Dry Goods, Clothing, Boots, Shoes, Groceries, Drugs,

Patent Medicines, Hardware, Seeds,

— AND —

FAMILY AND PLANTATION SUPPLIES.

11	To 1 Pa Pants		2 10	
	1 " Brogans		2 0 0	
	1 " Calf Shoes		3 50	
	14 Yds Osnaburg @ 17		2 38	
	10 " Stripes — 14	1 40	5 10

Recd Payment Wright & Moody

Clothing and supplies purchased by Joseph "FreeJoe" Harris on credit
was paid by the estate.

188

Received of Walter C Allen Ex of Jos. Harris
Deced ($20 00) Twenty Dollars for Surveying
& Dividing the Estate Lands
Oct 12th /875 -

              M.F. Leake

Payment was made to Millard F. Leake to survey the lands owned by Joseph "FreeJoe" Harris.

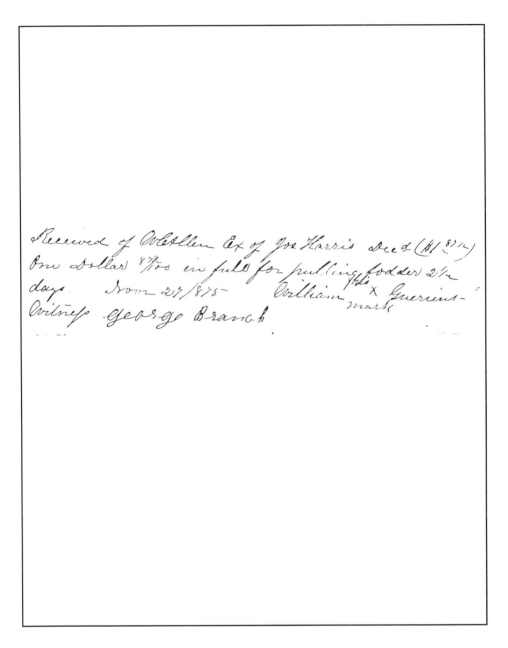

Received of Col Allen Ex of Jos Harris Dec d (A1 87 1/4)
One Dollar 8/100 in full for pulling fodder 2 1/2
days. Nov 27/875 — William his X Guerin
mark
Witness George Branch.

Payment was made from the Joseph "FreeJoe" Harris estate for services rendered.

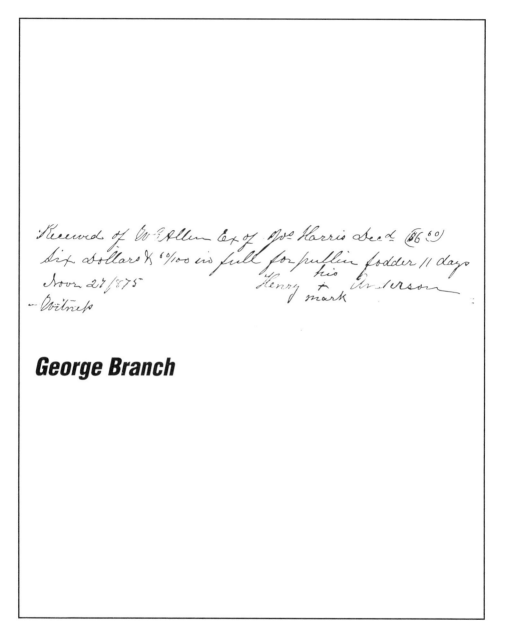

Received of W. E Allen Ex of Jos Harris decd ($6 50)
Six dollars & 50/100 in full for pullin fodder 11 days
Noov 27/875
— Witness

Henry his + mark Anderson

George Branch

Payment made from the estate of Joseph "FreeJoe" Harris
for services rendered.

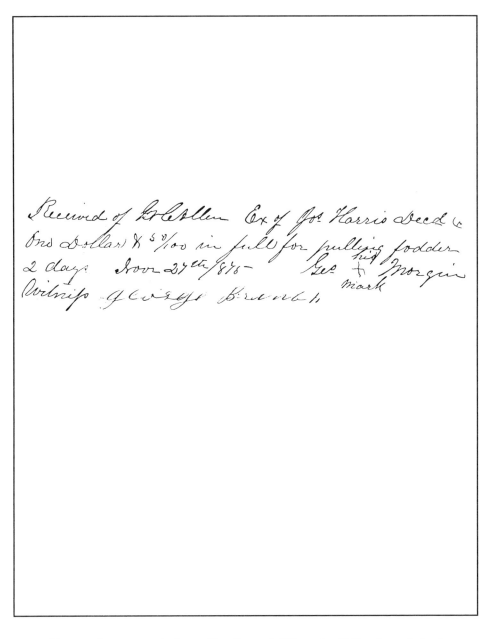

Received of Jno Allen Ex of Jos Harris Decd &
One Dollar & 50/100 in full for pulling fodder
2 days. Novr 27th/875 — Geo his Morgin
                                    +
                                  mark
Witness George Branch,

Payment was made from the Joseph "FreeJoe" Harris estate for services rendered.

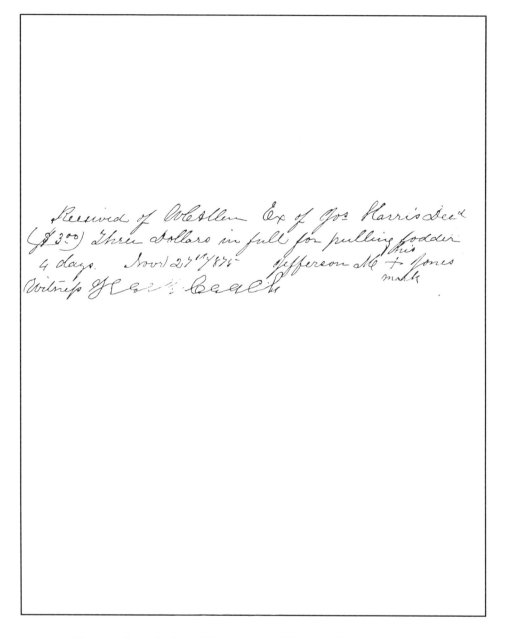

Received of W C Allen Ex of Jos Harris dec'd
($3.00) Three dollars in full for pulling fodder
4 days.   Nov'd 27th 1875   Jefferson M + Jones
                                              his
                                             mark
Witness J   Beall

**Payment made from the estate of Joseph "FreeJoe" Harris
for services rendered.**

Received of Wl Allen Ex of Jos Harris decd $... ..
in full for Carrying chain in division
of Land 2 days
Decr 15/1875   his
                              John + Lee
Witness   mark
M M...

**Payment made by the estate of Joseph "FreeJoe" Harris
for services rendered.**

Supplies for the Inn purchased on credit and paid by the estate of Joseph "FreeJoe" Harris.

1875 Jos Harris Estate Dr To Edward Ford
July To 4 days work @ 50 pr day $2.00
Received pay in full on above
Act- Through the hand of Wb Allen Ex
witness.   Decr 15th /1875-   Edward + Ford
George Branch   his
                                                mark

**Payment made by the estate of Joseph "FreeJoe" Harris
for services rendered.**

196

1875 Estate of Jos Harris Dr. To Jos Lewis
To 3½ days work $ 5.00
      Received pay in full on above act-
      Through the hands of WC Allen Ex
      Decr 15ᵗʰ 1875-   Joseph his X Lewis
                                        mark
Witness george Branch

**Payment made by the estate of Joseph "FreeJoe" Harris
for services rendered.**

Recived of Wt Allen Ext of Jos Harris decd ($19.00) in full for Services rendered on farm (picking Cotton & gathering Corn)
Decr/15th/875   Thos   his
                              + Anderson
                            mark
Witness
George Branch

**Payment from the estate of Joseph "FreeJoe" Harris
for services rendered.**

198

Received of Wr C Allen Ex of Jos Harris
dee't ($20 00/ Twenty Dollars for two
months work @ $18 00 pr month
Dec'r 15th/875   Henry + Anderson
                          his
Witness   mark
George Branch

**Payment made by the estate of Joseph "FreeJoe" Harris
for services rendered.**

Deer 16 1875 - Walter C Allen Ex of Jos Harris decd
          Dr To C E Williams
          " Lining Bagging & Ties for
          5 Bales Cotton $6 50   32 50
          Received pay on Above acr -
          Deer 16th 1875   C, E Williams

**Payment made by the estate of Joseph "FreeJoe" Harris
for services rendered.**

Received of Wt C Allen Ex of Jos Harris Dec'd ($2.00) Two Dollars in full for carrying the chain 2 days Surveying Land,
Dec'r 17/87 —   James + Royster
                                   his
                                   mark

Witness
T. E. Williams

Payment made by the estate of Joseph "FreeJoe" Harris for services rendered.

44.

W. C. Allen Ex' Jos. Harris

Bartlett Dec 23 1875

To Louisville & Nashville Railroad, Dr.

	For Transportation on the following articles of Freight, viz:	Weight.	Rate.	Freight.
B.	600 ft Lumber			
r,	2 doors 1 Bdl Sash			1 6 5
te	187			
om				
nsignor,		Charges advanced.		4 0
Bills payable in Bankable Funds.	Received Payment for the Company, [signature] Agent.	Total,		2 0 5

Freight for building supplies purchased by Joseph "FreeJoe" Harris on credit and paid by his estate.

Memphis, Tenn., Dec 20 1875

Mr. W. C. Allen

Bought of Harris, Mallory & Co.,

Successors to HARRIS, COCHRAN & CO.,

Wholesale Grocers & Cotton Factors,

erms Cash.   254 FRONT STREET, Star Building.

ALL REMITTANCES BY EXPRESS MUST BE PREPAID.

| 5 Kegs Nails 1/6/8/10 5 sacks 35 | 10 | 80 |
| 5 day. | 25 | 1 05 |

For Est Jos Harris.

Building supplies purchased by Joseph "FreeJoe" Harris on credit and paid by his estate.

203

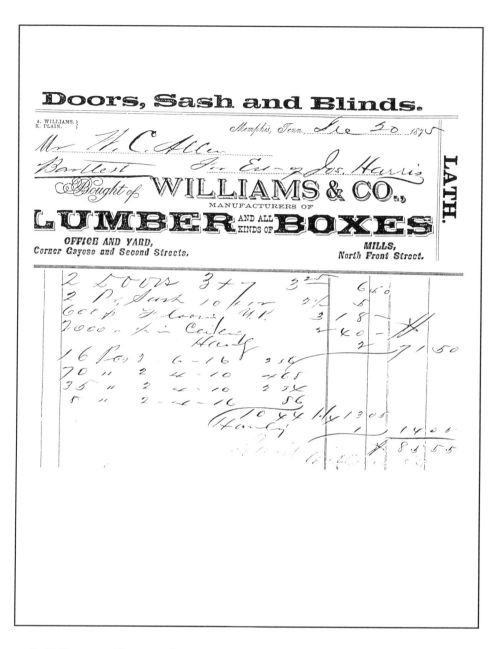

Building supplies purchased by Joseph "FreeJoe" Harris on credit and paid by his estate.

Received of Maitland Ex of Jno
J Harris Dec ($150⁰⁰) One hundred
and fifty Dollars in full for
Services rendered on farm during
the year 1875. Jan 1st 1876
Geo. Branch

**Payment by the estate of Joseph "FreeJoe" Harris
for services rendered.**

Received of Walter C Allen Exr Fifteen
Dollars in full for putting up one Back
Chimney on the Jo. Harris place for the
benefit of the Widow of Decd
Jan 1st 1876
J. H. Chason

Payment made by the estate of Joseph "FreeJoe" Harris for services rendered.

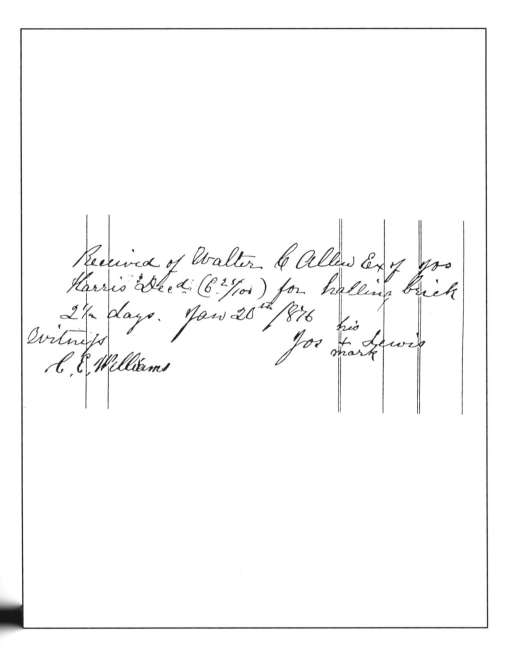

Received of Walter C Allen Ex of Jos
Harris Deed (6.25/100) for halling brick
2½ days. Jan 20th 1876
Witness   his
                              Jos + Lewis
C. E. Williams   mark

**Payment made by the estate of Joseph "FreeJoe" Harris
for services rendered.**

Jan 25, 1876 Col C Allen Exr of Jos Harris Decd Dr
        To N J Justice
  "   "   "   3000 Brick at $10 pr Thousand $ 30 50
Received pay on above act
        Jan 25 /876
                    N J Justice

**Building supplies purchased by Joseph "FreeJoe" Harris on credit
and paid by his estate.**

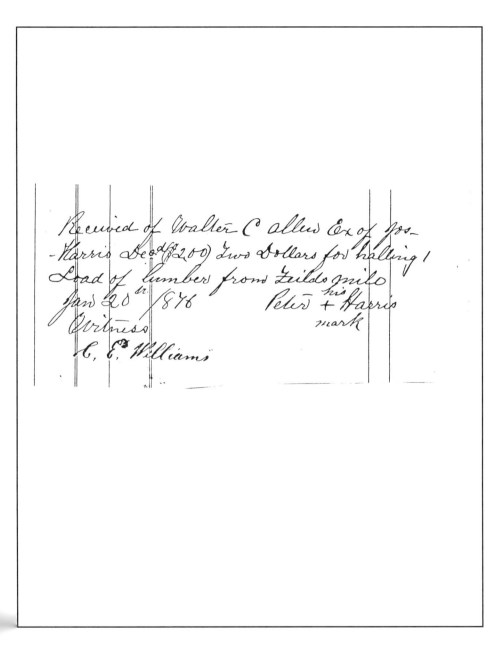

Received of Walter C Allen Ex of Jos-
-Harris Dec'd ($2.00) Two Dollars for halling 1
Load of lumber from Feilds mill
Jan 20th 1876   Peter + Harris
                                      his mark
Witness
C. E. Williams

**Payment made by the estate of Joseph "FreeJoe" Harris
for services rendered.**

209

Bartlett, Tenn., *Feb 8th* 187 6

Mr *W C Allen for Estate of Joseph Harris*

Bought of WRIGHT, SHELBY & SHOTWELL,

DEALERS IN

Dry Goods, Clothing, Boots, Shoes, Groceries, Drugs,

Patent Medicines, Hardware, Seeds,

—AND—

FAMILY AND PLANTATION SUPPLIES.

2	Door Locks	@ 100	2	00
2	Pr Butts	" 25		50
2½	Doz Screws	" 10		25
			2	75

Payd   Wright & Moody

Building supplies purchased by Joseph "FreeJoe" Harris on credit
and paid by his estate.

Received of Walter C Allen Ex of Jos Harris
Dec'd ($97.ºº) Ninty seven Dollars for building
Dwelling House, Store or Smoke House &
Hen House for Widow of Dec'd as Named
in Marridge Contract- of Said Jos Harris
& Millie Harris.
     Feb 19 1876   Monroe ^{his} + Guerint-
                                mark
Attest-
Randle Davis

**The estate of Joseph "FreeJoe" Harris honors the prenuptial
agreement signed by Joseph "FreeJoe" Harris and Millie Wash
on October 1, 1869.**

211

Received of W.C. Allen Executor of
Joseph Harris Decd ($20⁰⁰)
Twenty Dollars for building one
stable & corn crib for the benefit
of the widow of Decd
April 7th 1876

                        his
              Monroe + Gurient
                        mark
Witness
    Charl Allen

The estate of Joseph "FreeJoe" Harris pays for the building of a stable and corn crib for the widow of Joseph "FreeJoe" Harris, Milly Wash.

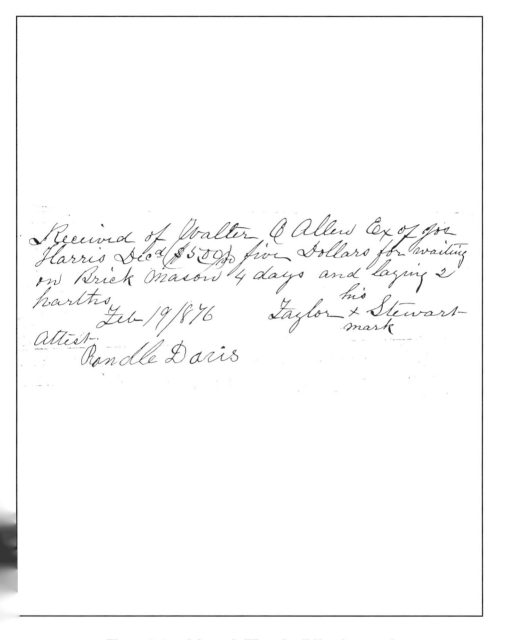

Received of Walter C Allen Ex of Jos
Harris Decd ($5.00) five Dollars for waiting
on Brick Mason 4 days and laying 2
harths
          Feb 19/876   Taylor + Stewart
                                        his   mark
Attest.
        Randle Davis

The estate of Joseph "FreeJoe" Harris pays for building related services.

57.

District No. 8   Ward No. _____   Folio, 7   *Memphis, Tenn.,* Apr 18th 1876

Joseph Harris Estate

To State and County Taxes for 1875.

Acres.	Lot.	Block.		VALUATION.
				$	$
17			Jms Jms Williams Royster Webber	2200	

RATE OF TAX :

40	State,	8	80
25	County,	5	50
5	Judgments,	1	10
5	Courthouse Improvement Tax,	1	10
15	School,	3	30
15	Courthouse Tax,	3	30
10	M. & O. R. R. Coupon Tax,	2	20
10	Poor and Pest House Tax,	2	20
$2	Poll,		
$2 3	Dog,	6	—
	Penalty,	33	50

Received Payment,

A. E. Frankland
C. M. Poital   Tax Collector.
                                Deputy.

Taxes paid by the estate of Joseph "FreeJoe" Harris.

214

W C Allen Ex of Jos Harris decd Dr
1875   To Robt Ford
July   To 3 days work at $1.00 $3.00
                Recived three Dollars in
                full on above act from
                W C Allen Ex
Witness   May 19th/1876   Robert + Ford
A J Fletcher.   mark

The estate of Joseph "FreeJoe" Harris pays for services rendered.

Allen Ex of Jos Harris
Dr To Geo Branch
lling Lumber and .
6 days $2.50 for day $15.00
ed May 12th 1876 of
en En fifteen Dollars
ove Act
Geo Branch

The estate of Joseph "FreeJoe" Harris pays for services rendered.

District No. _8_ Ward No. _____ Folio, _110_

Memphis, Tenn., _Dec 26_ 1876

M _Jos. Harris Est_ _____

To State and County Taxes for 1876.

Acres.	Lot.	Block.		VALUATION.
67			Joins Jeff Jones & othrs	1850

RATE OF TAX:			
40	State,	7 40	
35	County,	6 48	
15	Judgments,	2 78	
15	School,	2 77	
10	Court House,	1 85	
10	M. & R. R. R. Tax,	1 85	
5	M. & O. R. R. Coupon Tax,	93	
5	Poor and Pest House Tax,	92	
$2	Poll,		24 98
$2	Dog,.		
$6	Bitch,		
	Interest,		
	Penalty,		
	Received Payment,	J J Rawlings	Trustee.
		N H _____	Deputy.

Taxes paid by the estate of Joseph "FreeJoe" Harris.

Executed August 13 1877 on George Branch and
wife Marthie Branch. Jeff M Jones and wife
Lettie Jones. — Ford infant child of Robert an
Mary Ford, Peter Harriss. Rhoda Green
Joe Lewis, Frank Leake, Milly Harriss an
James Harris by making known to them cont
of within Notice C L Anderson Shy
By D L McGowian Dd

The heirs of Joseph "FreeJoe" Harris are summoned for
the reading of his will.

218

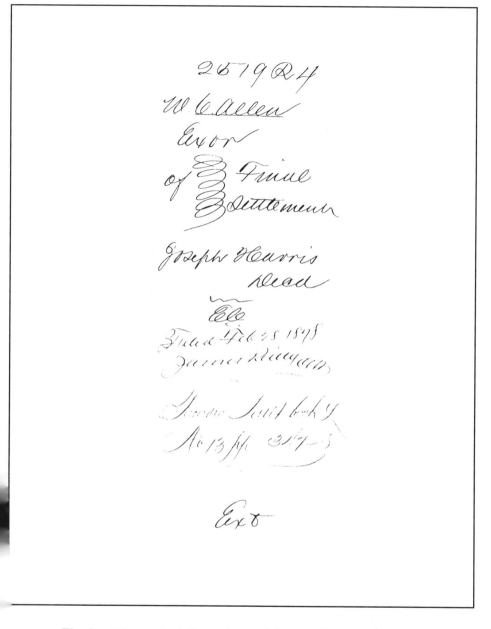

Final settlement of the estate of Joseph "FreeJoe" Harris.

and that no exceptions have been filed thereto.   It is therefore ordered

that the said settlement be, and the same is hereby in all things confirmed,

and that the same be recorded in the Settlement Records of this Court

And it appearing that W. C. Allen the Exer.

has this day paid into Court the sum of

$508 ᵒᵒ the distributive share of

the Heirs of Mary Hood, decd. it is therefore

ordered that the said fund be distributed, &

W. C. Allen having this day qualified as

Guardian of Elijah Hood one of the Children

of said Mary Hood decd. who is entitled

to ¼ of said fund the said Amn of ¼

Final settlement of the estate of Joseph "FreeJoe" Harris.

State of Tennessee, } I _W. C. Allen_
County of Shelby.
solemnly swear that the foregoing settlement of my accounts as _Exor_ of Estate
of _Joseph Harris_ exhibits a full, true and just statement of each and
every of the assets of said _____ Estate, with which
I should be charged, and of the credits to which I am entitled, to the best of my knowledge
and belief—so help me God.

W. C. Allen

Subscribed and Sworn to before me, this _6_ _day of_ _Febury_ 187 _8_

James Reilly Clerk.

By _Hugh D. Cullen_ Deputy Clerk.

Finalizing the estate of Joseph "FreeJoe" Harris.

221

IN THE PROBATE COURT.

No. 26519   Record No. 1

Wm. C. Allen
Exor

OF	ORDER Confirming Settlement, Etc.

Joseph O'Harris
decd

Entered March 4 187 5

Minute Book 20 349

Final settlement of the estate of Joseph "FreeJoe" Harris.

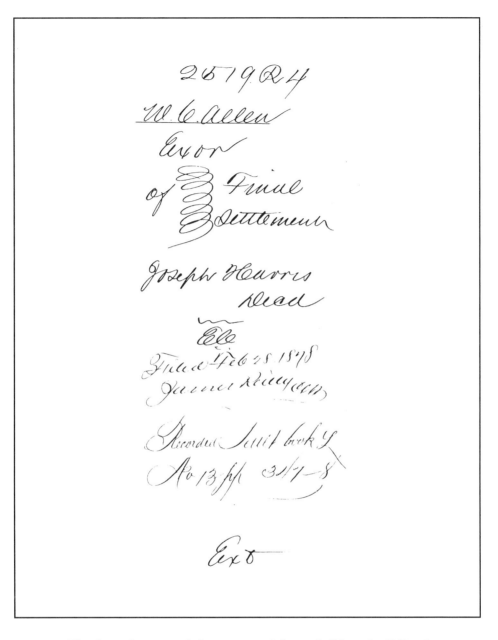

Final settlement of the estate of Joseph "FreeJoe" Harris.

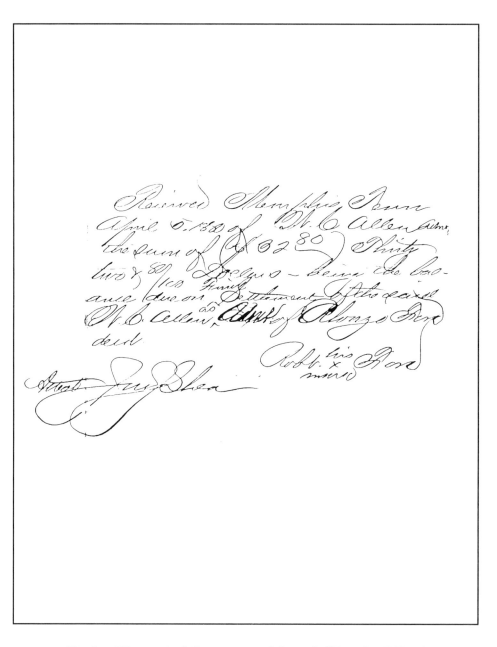

Final settlement of the estate of Joseph "FreeJoe" Harris.

Received of W. C. Allen Administrator of Alonzo Ford ($200.00) Two hundred Dollars in part of My interest in said Estate

Robt ×(his mark) Ford

Final settlement of the estate of Joseph "FreeJoe" Harris.

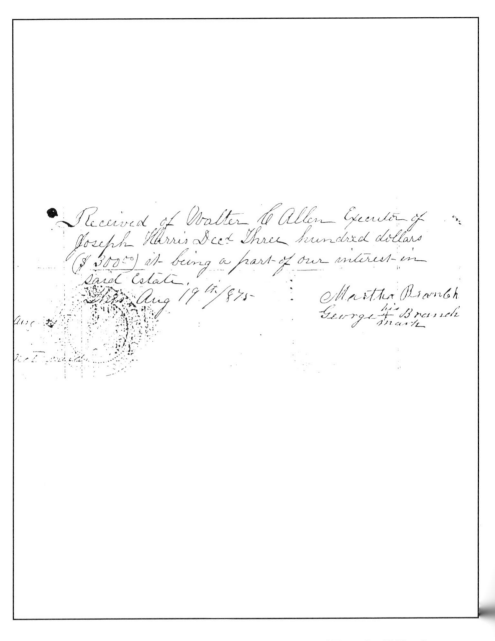

Received of Walter C Allen Executor of
Joseph Harris Dec^d Three hundred dollars
($300.00) it being a part of our interest in
said Estate. This Aug 19th/875

Martha Branch
George + Branch
his mark

Final settlement of the estate of Joseph "FreeJoe" Harris.

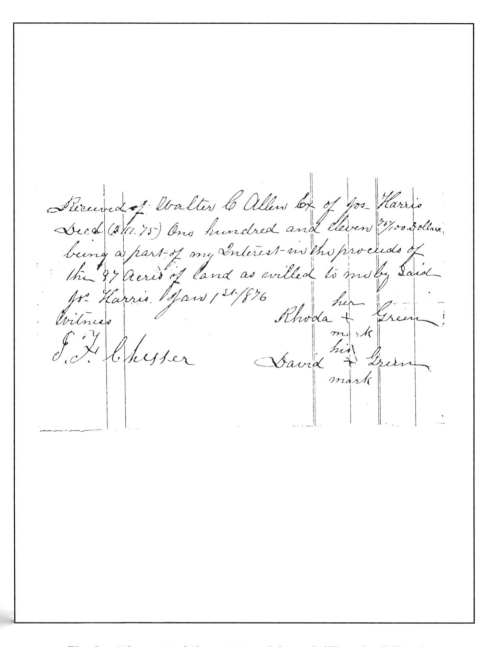

Received of Walter C Allen Ex of Jos Harris
Decd ($111.75) One hundred and eleven 75/100 Dollars.
being a part of my Interest in the proceeds of
the 97 Acres of land as willed to me by said
Jos. Harris. Jany 1st/876

Witness   her
                              Rhoda + Green
                                              mark

J. F. Chester   his
                              David + Green
                                              mark

Final settlement of the estate of Joseph "FreeJoe" Harris.

Honorable J E R Ray Judg of the Probate Court of Shelby County Tennesee, By request of Robert Ford Father of Alonzo Ford deceased an infant child 16 months old, the petitioner W C Allen prays your Honor that he be granted Letters of Administration on said Alonzo Fords Estate Consisting of Personal property to the amount of Two Hundred and fifty four 00/100 Dollars ($254 00/100).

March 4th /878   Walter C Allen

Sworn to & subscribed before me
This 4th day of March 1878.
            D Cough D Cushman D C

Final settlement of the estate of Joseph "FreeJoe" Harris.

Honorable J E R Ray Judge of the Probate
Court of Shelby County Tennessee
The undersigned feeling his incompetency and
not being able to give Bond prays Your
Honor that you appoint W C Allen Guardian
+ Administrator of the Estate of his infant
Child Alonzo Ford who died during the
month of Oct 1875 aged 16 months, said
Child was the son of Mary Ford and
one of the Heirs of Joseph Harris died
Feb 13th 1878
Witness,   his
                    Robert + Ford
      his   mark
Joseph + Lewis
      mark

Final settlement of the estate of Joseph "FreeJoe" Harris.

Received of W. C. Allen Executor of the Estate of Joseph Harris deceased one hundred and fifteen Dollars ($115#) it being a part of my interest in said Estate.

$115#

Virginia Phillips
Wesley Phillips

State of Michigan)
Kalamazoo County)

On this 19th day of Jany AD 1877. personally came before me a Notary Public in & for said County & acknowledged Virginia Phillips & Wesley Phillips who severally acknowledged the execution of the above receipt. Wesley Phillips

_____
Notary Public

Final settlement of the estate of Joseph "FreeJoe" Harris.

230

Received of W C Allen Executor of Joseph Harris Deceased ($225 7/100) Two Hundred and twenty five Dollars being a part of our distribution shars in said Estate This March 16th 1876

Jef M^{his} ✗ Jones

Jette Jones ^{her mark}

Final settlement of the estate of Joseph "FreeJoe" Harris.

Final settlement of the estate of Joseph "FreeJoe" Harris.

232

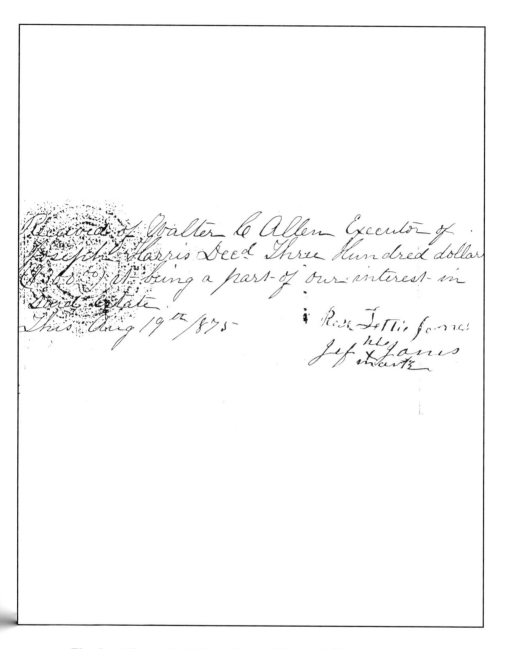

Received of Walter C Allen Executor of
Joseph Harris Decd Three Hundred dollars
($300.00) it being a part of our interest in
said Estate
This Aug 19th /875 -

Rec Lottie James

Jef X James
  his
  mark

Final settlement of the estate of Joseph "FreeJoe" Harris.

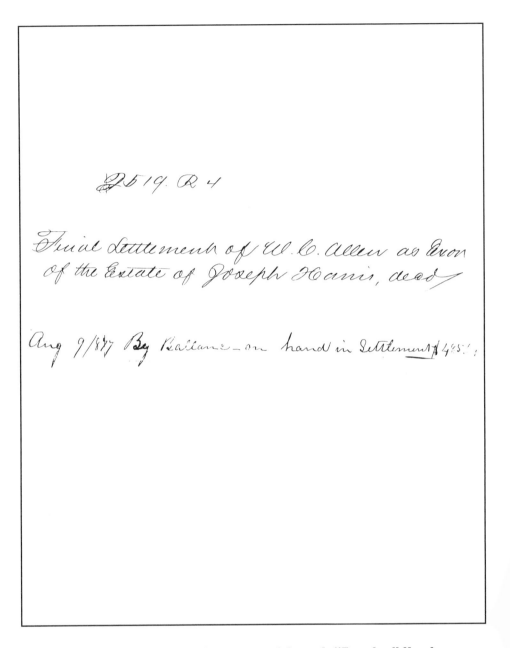

2519. R 4

Final Settlement of W. C. Allen as Exon
of the Estate of Joseph Harris, dead

Aug 9/1877 By Balance on hand in Settlement $495.00

Final settlement of the estate of Joseph "FreeJoe" Harris.

" " " To Cash paid C. [?] Court-Clerk on Settlement $19.50
" Costs present settlement   9.75
Balance on hand   457.39

Real Estate a[?]h (4th Clause of will)   485.64
By Ballance on hand in last-settlement 54.75
Dec'd 15/877 By Cash received of Milley Harrison Land $33.34
" " " " " " Peter Leake " " 153.32
" " " " " " Jos. Lewis & Frank Leake 191.65
" " " " " " Rhoda Green 114.94
                                          $ 548.00

Final settlement of the estate of Joseph "FreeJoe" Harris.

235

To Ballance on hand in last Settlement $_____

ct/877 To Amt Paid Peter Leake $123.35

"   "   "   "   " Rhoda Green   123.35

"   "   "   "   " Joe Lewis & Frank Leake 123.35

Ballance   178.00

                                        $ 548.05

Final settlement of the estate of Joseph "FreeJoe" Harris.

236

The State of Tennessee,

To the Sheriff of Shelby County:

SUMMON *George Branch, wife Martha*
Jeff M. Jones, wife Letty, — Ford
infant child of Robt & Mary Ford, Peter Harris,
Rhoda Green, Jos Lewis, & Frank Leake
Milly Harris, and James Harris

to appear before me, at my office in the City of Memphis, Tenn., on the _31st_ day of
August 187_7_ at 10 o'clock A. M., *To be present*
at the stating of a settlement of
the accounts of W. C. Allen
as Executor of the will of
Joseph Harris, decd

on behalf of the ~~~~~~~ and this you shall in no wise omit, under
penalty prescribed by law. Herein fail not, and have you then and there this writ.

Witness, JAMES REILLY, Clerk of said Court, at office, in the City of
Memphis, this _9_ day of _August_ 187_7_, and
_102_ Year of American Independence.

James Reilly _____ Clerk.

By *Hugh B. Cullen* D. C.

Final settlement of the estate of Joseph "FreeJoe" Harris.

W. C. Allen Exor, makes the following statement that under the will the residue of the personal estate after the payment of debts &c was to be divided among his four children towit, Martha Mary, Lettie and Cornelius, share + share alike, under said clause there remained for distribution the sum of $2032.39
Each share onefourth being asfollows.

Martha Branch	508.09
Cornelius Harris	508.10
Lettie Jones	508.10
minor Heirs of Mary Ford	508.10

to each of the adults the Exor haspaid $500. and they will haveto refund to him $16.90 each.

Mary Ford daughter of Jos Harris + one of the devisees above named died before the death of Jos Harris + left surviving her two children both of whom survived the Testator Jos Harris. Since said Testators death however one has died towit Ford, the other Elijah Ford is a minor aged 6 years + three

Final settlement of the estate of Joseph "FreeJoe" Harris.

238

The Ex'or is advised that Admn
is necessary on the former and a
Gon for the latters estate.

As to the Balance of $ 178.00
due by Ex'or on a/c of
Real Estate Sold under
4th Clause of the Will
of Jos Harris the parties
named in said clause
&/c are entitled as
follows.

    Virginia Phillips 137. 02
    Peter Harris Paid Feb 18/78 Settle   13, 66
    Rhoda Green Paid Feb 18/78 " "   13 66
    Joseph Lewis & Frand Leake Paid Feb 18/78   13. 66
                 $ 178. 00

March 11. 1878. The Ex'or has this day paid into
Court the sum of $508 10 being the amount
due the Heirs of Mary Ford, dec'd, which
is subject to the orders of your Hon Court
          James Riddy Clk
          By Hugh B. Cullen D.C.

Final settlement of the estate of Joseph "FreeJoe" Harris.

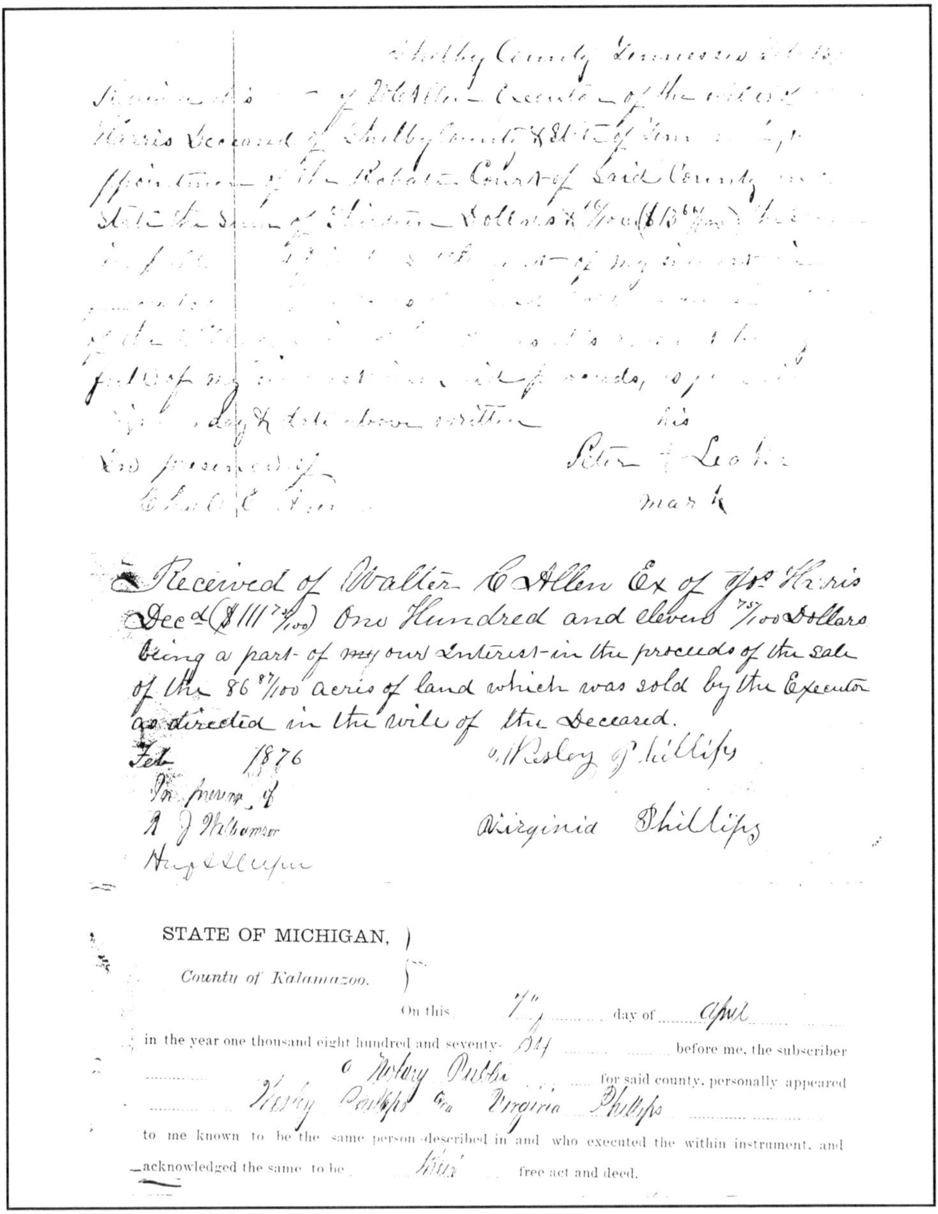

Shelby County Tennessee [illegible]

[illegible] of W. C. Allen Executor of the will of [illegible] Harris Deceased of Shelby County [illegible] appointment of the Probate Court of said County [illegible] the sum of [illegible] Dollars & 66/100 ($13 66/100) [illegible]

[illegible] day & date above written

his
Peter [illegible]
mark

In presence of
[illegible]

Received of Walter C Allen Ex of Jos. Harris Decd ($111 75/100) One Hundred and eleven 75/100 Dollars being a part of my own Interest in the proceeds of the sale of the 86 87/100 acres of land which was sold by the Executor as directed in the will of the Deceased.

Feb 1876 Wesley Phillips

In presence of
R J Williamson Virginia Phillips
Hugh [illegible]

STATE OF MICHIGAN,
County of Kalamazoo.

On this 7th day of April in the year one thousand eight hundred and seventy-six before me, the subscriber a Notary Public for said county, personally appeared Wesley Phillips and Virginia Phillips to me known to be the same person described in and who executed the within instrument, and acknowledged the same to be their free act and deed.

Final settlement of the estate of Joseph "FreeJoe" Harris.

Received of Walter C Allen
Ex of Jos Harris Dec'd ($115 00)
One hundred and fifteen
Dollars being a part of our
interest in said Estate
Decr 15th /876
Witness   Joe his + Lewis
                        mark

F.R. Teate

Received of Walter C Allen Executor of Joseph
Harris Dec'd One Hundred & twenty three 35/100 Doll.
($123.35) it being a part of my Interest in said
Joseph Harris Estate   February 6th / 878 her
Test   Rhoda + Green
A J Justice   mark

Shelby County Tenn Feb /878
Received at is date of Walter C Allen Executor
of the will of Joseph Harris deceased of the State,
County & State of Tennessee, under appointment
from the Probate Court of said County and
State the Sum of Thirteen Dollars and
66/100 ($13 66/100) the Same being in full and
final settlement of my interest in proceeds
of 86 87/100 Acres of land Sold under directi
of the 4th Clause of the will of said Joseph
Harris, this amount being in full of my

Final settlement of the estate of Joseph "FreeJoe" Harris.

241

Received of Walter C Allen Executor of
Joseph Harris Dec'd One Hundred &
twenty three 35/100 Dollars ($123 35/100)
it being a part of my Interest in Said
Joseph Harris Estate. Feb 4th /878

Test—
N. _____, justice

Peter ____ Lewis
his
mark

Shelby County Tenn Feb 13th
Received this date of Walter C Allen Executor
of the wife of Joseph Harris deceased of the
County of Shelby & State of Tennessee, and
_____ from the Probate Court of said
County and State, the Sum of Thirteen ____
and 66/100 ($13 66/100) the Same being in full and
final settlement of our ____ the proceeds of
86 ___/100 ____ of land sold under direction of
the 4th Clause of the wile of Said Joseph
Harris, this amount being in full of ____
said proceeds, as per said wile
Signed day & date above written
_____

in presence of
his
Robert + Ford
mark

his
Joseph + Lewis
mark

Final settlement of the estate of Joseph "FreeJoe" Harris.

1875

Dec 15
1877
Jan. 11
1876 Dec 15

„ Compensation to Executor for
making Sale 27.00
Balance 54.75
988.75

1870

189.60
38.48

Rhoda Green 115.00
988.75

Balance due on this A/c

Final settlement of the estate of Joseph "FreeJoe" Harris.

243

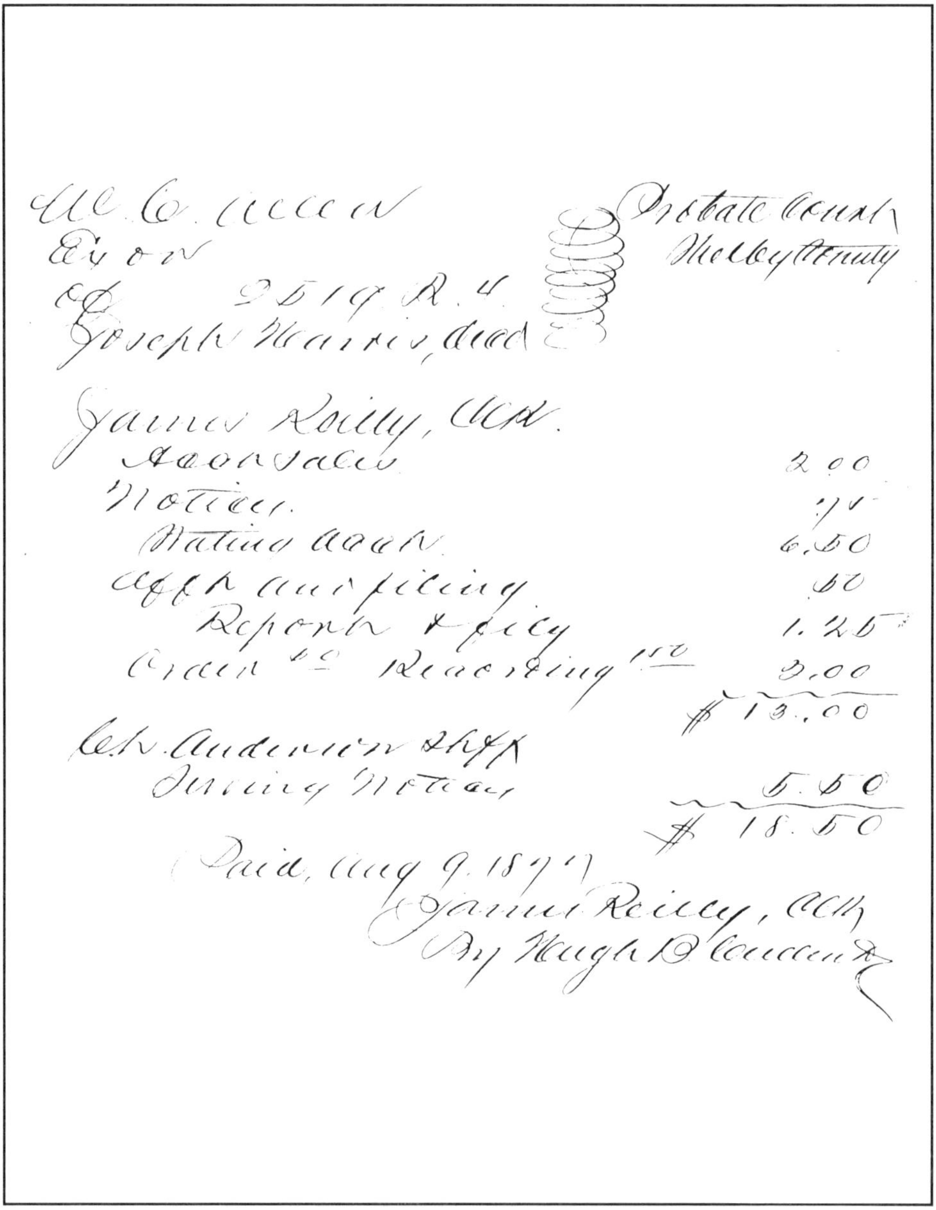

W. C. Allen
Ex or
of 2519 R. 4.
Joseph Harris, dead

Probate Court
Shelby County

James Reilly, Clk.
Appr. sales 2.00
Notice .75
Writing appr. 6.50
Affd and filing .50
Report & filing 1.25
Order & Recording etc 3.00
$13.00

W. H. Anderson Shff
Serving Notice 5.50
$18.50

Paid, Aug 9. 1877
James Reilly, Clk
By Hugh B. [illegible]

Final settlement of the estate of Joseph "FreeJoe" Harris.

Kalamazoo, Mich, Feb 27, 1878

Received this date of Watt C. Allen, Executor of the will of Joseph Harris, deceased of the County of Shelby, and State of Tennessee, under appointment from the Probate Court of said County and State, the sum of One Hundred and fifty Seven 10/100 ($157 10/100) Dollars the same being in full and final Settlement of my interest in proceeds of 86 8/100 acres of land sold under direction of the 4th Clause of the will of said Joseph Harris, this amount being in full of my interest in said proceeds, as per said will.

Signed day & date above written

W. Wesley Phillips

Virginia Phillips

In presence of
R. J. Williamson
Hugh Sleeper

Final settlement of the estate of Joseph "FreeJoe" Harris.

245

Final settlement of the estate of Joseph "FreeJoe" Harris.

I, **HENRY S. SLEEPER,** Clerk of the County of Kalamazoo, and of the Circuit Court in and for said County, do hereby certify that _____ whose genuine signature appears to the foregoing _____ was at the time of signing the same a Notary Public in and for said county duly commissioned, and sworn; that all his official acts, as such, are entitled to full faith and credit, and that the said Circuit Court is a Court of Record having general jurisdiction.

IN WITNESS WHEREOF, I have hereunto set my hand and affixed the seal o said Court, this_____ day of _____ 187__

_____ _Clerk._

Final settlement of the estate of Joseph "FreeJoe" Harris.

247

said County *Wesley Phillips and Virginia Phillips*

the within named bargainers with whom I am personally acquainted, and who acknowledged that *they* executed the within instrument for the purposes therein contained

And *Virginia Phillips, wife* of the said *Wesley Phillips* having appeared before me privately and apart from her husband, the said *Wesley Phillips* acknowledged the execution of the said *Instrument* to have been done by *her* freely, voluntarily and understandingly, without compulsion or constraint from *her* said husband, and for the purposes therein expressed.

Witness, *R. J. Williamson* Notary *Public* of said County at office, this *27* day of *February* 187*8*

Robert J. Williamson
Notary Public
Kalamazoo Co
Mich

Final settlement of the estate of Joseph "FreeJoe" Harris.

248

PART IV
Exihibit

"FreeJoe"
The Renaissance Man
1796-1875
Exhibit

This exhibit is about a man and his times. There is one word that best describes Joseph "FreeJoe" Harris. That word is family.

When Joseph Harris received his freedom in 1832, he could have gone to the free state of Pennsylvania or north of the border to Canada, but he elected to stay with his family and travel deep into the bowels of slavery. Joseph Harris believed in the oldest human institution. Families make up the basis of every society. The family is the means for producing children and continuing the human race. The family provides protection and early training of infants and the family sets up a division of labor so that each contributes something.

Most of us belong to two families during our lifetime. The first as children and the second as parents. We are born into the first family and we establish the second one.

This exihibit produces personal dignity by showing people that they have treasures within themselves, histories worth harvesting. Through geneology, the exhibit provides a place to move forward from and inspiration to flourish, which in turn creates family pride and community betterment. Families are forever.

Simon Jackson, Jr. is the son of the late Clara Zelda Moore Jackson and Simon Jackson, Sr.

Jackson was born and raised in Eads, Tennessee in Fayette County. He graduated from Fayette-Ware High School.

Oldest standing brick structure in West Tennessee.

Jackson in his workshop.

Jackson works as a maintenance technician at Hampton Inn in Memphis. In addition, he works as an artist recreating detailed replicas of family homes, landmarks and the natural enviroment.

Since the age of 18, Jackson has been horning his art skills which is a God given talent. He never had any formal art training. His lifelike minature artwork has been featured in libraries, museums and banks, as well as newspapers and magazines in Memphis, Nashville, Chattanooga, Atlanta and San Pedro, California.

Harris Homestead House.

THE SEARCH FOR FREE JOE

Following are the descriptions of the displays that make up this exhibit.

1.) Introduction to the exhibit: A brief summary describing the nature of the exhibit.

2.) Emancipation of Joseph "FreeJoe" Harris: (1832) This document shows a description of Joseph, as well as his age when he was freed from slavery on September 5th,1832.

3.) The purchase of Fanny and Virginia: (1834) This document shows Joseph purchasing the freedom of his wife Fanny and sixteen month old daughter Virginia from Samuel Leake for $300.

4.) The purchase of Adeline "Lettie" Harris: (1840) Joseph purchased a 10 year old daughter from Samuel Leake for $300.

5.) The purchase of Susan "Sucky" Harris: (1856) Joseph purchased his oldest daughter from Bennett and Frances C. Bagby for $900. Bennett Bagby was the son-in-law and Frances C. Bagby was the daughter of Samuel and Sarah Leake.

6.) Prenupial Agreement: (1869) This document was drawn up prior to Joseph's marriage to Millie Wash, his second wife. Fanny, his first wife had died in 1865 during the mourning period for Abraham Lincoln.

7.) Gray's Creek Missionary Baptist Church: (1843) This church was renovated by Joseph Harris and he became its first minister in February of 1843. Prior to that time, the whites who follow the religious teachings of Alexander Campbell used it for worship services. Campbell was considered the greatest religious leader of the 1800's.

8.) Stagecoach Line and Inn: (1840-1929) Joseph Harris owned the stagecoach line that ran from Bolivar, Tennessee to Memphis, with an occasional trip to Jackson, Tennessee. He owned the stagecoach Inn at the corner of Highway 64 and Airline road. Many travelers would eat, have a good wash and stay overnight. After his death in 1875, his daughter Martha and her husband George Branch ran the Inn until the stagecoach line was disbanded.

9.) Census of 1850,1860 and 1870: These records show the Harris family. The 1850 census was the first census to show entire families and Joseph's family was the first complete family of African Americans found in Shelby County, Tennessee. His family appeared in the 1860 census.

That was the last appearance of his wife Fanny. In 1870, he appears with his second wife, Millie.

10.) Agricultural Census of 1850,1860 and 1870: These records show what Joseph raised and grew on his land. These records correspond to the population census records.

11.) Land purchases: (1834) This was Joseph's first land purchase. The purchase was made on the 20th of July, 1834 from T.R. Royster. Other land purchases are included.

12.) Land purchases: (1849) This land purchase was made from Richard Leake shortly before his death. Other land purchases are included.

13.) Samuel and Sarah Leake: (Pictures) Samuel Leake was Fanny's master and the master of all the children she had while still a slave. Samuel was also Joseph's sponsor. Free persons of color were required to have sponsors prior to the emancipation. Little is known of Sarah other than her maiden name was Johnson.

14.) Will of Samuel Leake: (1855) The will of Samuel Leake makes reference to Joseph Harris and other children of Joseph and Fanny Harris.

15.) Will of Sarah Leake: (1873) Sarah was the wife of Samuel Leake and mother of Dr. Virginius Leake. Her will reveals the names of many descendants that live in east Shelby County, Tennessee today.

16.) Will of John Harris Sr.: (1843) John Harris's Sr. was Joseph's father. A purchase from John Harris's estate indicates that Joseph did return to Goochland County, Virginia during that period. These records show that slaves were a plantation owner's most valued property.

17.) Martha Harris-Branch: (Picture) A daughter of Joseph and Fanny Harris. Martha married George Branch. After Joseph died, she and George ran the Inn, the stagecoach stop and moved into the house that Joseph once occupied.

18.) Oldest brick structure in West Tennessee: (1833-35) This house was built by Joseph Harris. This Tidewater style of house is out of place in West Tennessee. It is known to exist in Maryland and old Virginia.

19.) Dr. Virginius and Martha Leake: (Picture) Dr. Virginius Leake was the son of Samuel and Sarah Leake. His wife Martha Feild-Leake was a descendant of Thomas Jefferson. After the emancipation, Dr. Leake create a school to teach the newly freed slaves how to read, write and do arithmetic. In 1872 he ran for public office with the support of Joseph Harris and the newly freed slaves. He was elected as a Senator to the 38th General Assembly.

20.) GreenLevel" : (Picture) This house was renovated by Joseph Harris shortly after Dr. Virginius Leake purchased it from Bennett and Frances C. Bagby in 1850. During the Civil War, the house served as a hospital for Confederate soldiers. 119 wounded soldiers were brought to Greenlevel after the Battle of Shiloh .Blood stains on the floor of the upstairs hallway are an indication of where the operations were per-formed. The house is surrounded by unmarked graves of Confederate soldiers. This house has been placed on the National Register.

21.) Phoebe Anna Jones: (Picture) this is a daughter of Jefferson M. and Adeline "Lettie" Harris-Jones. She was a granddaughter of Joseph and Fanny Harris.

22.) Cornelius and Emma Jones-Harris: (Picture) Cornelius was the son of Joseph and Fanny Harris. He was also the named executor of Joseph Harris's estate. Emma Jones-Harris was the daughter of Jefferson M. and Adeline "Lettie" Jones. She was a granddaughter of Joseph and Fanny Harris. Cornelius and Emma were not only husband and wife, they were uncle and niece.

23.) Will of Richard Leake: (1849) Richard Leake was the brother of Samuel Leake. Joseph is mentioned in Richard's will. This document also reveals the names, gender and ages of the 29 slaves that Richard owned at the time of his death. This information corresponds to the slave schedule of 1850.

24.) Wesley and Virginia Harris-Phillips: (Picture) Wesley moved to Indiana from Georgia when he was a young lad and Virginia was taken to Indiana and enrolled in a boarding school by her father, Joseph Harris. While there she and Wesley met and got married on November 15th, 1849. They moved with their family to Kalamazoo, Michigan during the middle of the Civil War in 1862. They had a total of 12 children.

25.) The daughters of Virginia and Wesley Phillips: (Picture) The grand daughters of Joseph and Fanny Harris.

26.) The sons of Virginia and Wesley Phillips: (Picture) Grandsons of Joseph and Fanny Harris. All of the grandsons played the violin. Sylvester was the singer. His most popular song was " sleeper in the down".

27.) Will of Joseph Harris: (1875) Joseph's will was probated beginning in 1875. His estate remained open for three years.

28.) The inventory of Joseph Harris's estate: (1875) an inventory was taken of everything that Joseph owned and a value was placed on each item.

29.) The sale of Joseph Harris's personal property: (1875) All the items sold were described, along with the price paid for each item and the name of the person who made the purchase.

30.) This is a continuation of display # 29.

31.) The sale and disbursement of the Joseph Harris estate: (1875) This is a continuation of displays # 29 and 30. In addition, cash disbursements are made to family members.

32.) The estate of Joseph Harris: (1875) This part of the estate deals with the disbursement of money awarded to Mary Harris-Ford, the deceased daughter of Joseph and Fanny Harris, that died seven weeks before Joseph did, and money awarded to Alonzo Ford, the son of Mary and Robert Ford, grandson of Joseph and Fanny Harris, who died later that year in October, 1875.

33.) Continuation of #32.

34.) Probate Records: (1875-1878) These displays consists of bills submitted to the estate for payment. These are bills submitted by workers who sign for their money with "X's", Joseph's final doctor's bill, property tax bills, freight bills for lumber shipped by the railroads, bills for building materials purchased on credit in Memphis and Bartlett, Tennessee prior to 1875 and a bill for the labor to build Millie a log cabin per the prenupial agreement of October 1, 1869.

35.) Continuation of # 34

36.) Continuation of # 34

37.) Continuation of # 34

38.) Continuation of # 34

39.) Continuation of # 34

40.) Continuation of # 34

41.) My name is Harris: (1878) An assumption was made that since Peter Harris, the oldest child and son of Joseph and Fanny Harris, was born a slave on Samuel Leake's plantation, his name was Peter Leake. Court records were changed to reflect the fact that his name was Harris, Peter Harris.

42.) A kiss for "FreeJoe": (1997) the grandparents of Lucy Claxton, a resident of Fayette County, Tennessee, knew Joseph "FreeJoe" Harris. She recounts some stories told to her by her grandparents about FreeJoe.

43.) Searching for "FreeJoe": (1984-Present) Newspaper articles documenting the research done by Genealogist, Author Earnest Edward Lacey, the great, great, great grandson of Joseph "FreeJoe" and Fanny Harris.

44.) Description of the "FreeJoe" Homestead House and its contents: (1997) Self explanatory

45.) Freejoe" Homestead House: (1997)(3-Dimensional) The first and only log cabin built by artist Simon Jackson. This is a down scale version of the house that Joseph "FreeJoe " Harris lived in at the time of his death in 1875.

46.) The Book: (1996) Every life is a story. This is the life story of Joseph " FreeJoe" Harris.

47.) Marriage license of Joseph and Fanny Harris: (1835) Joseph and Fanny were the first couple of color to get married in Shelby County, Tennessee.

48.) Marriage license of Joseph and Millie Wash: (1869) Joseph and Millie were married on October 4th, 1869.

49.) The John Gray House (1998)(3-dimensional down scale version of the actual house) The first and only complete brick house built by artist Simon Jackson. This is a down scale version of the house built by Joseph "FreeJoe" Harris in the early 1830's.

50.) Shofar (1998) (3-dimensional down scale version of the actual horn) A type of Ram's horn blown by the stagecoach drivers that drove for Joseph "FreeJoe" Harris.

51.) The Stagecoach (1998) (3-dimensional down scale version of the actual stagecoach) This is the first and only stagecoach built by artist Simon Jackson. This is the type of stagecoach used by Joseph "FreeJoe" Harris when he made his runs to Bolivar, Jackson and Memphis, Tennessee.

52.) Clothing.(1998) (3-Dimensional) this is the type of work clothing wore during that time period.

53.) Peter and Laura Ann Jones-Harris (Picture) Peter Harris, the oldest child and son of Joseph "FreeJoe" and Fanny Harris, was born in Goochland

County, Virginia in 1823. He was Samuel Leake's manservant and was married to Laura Ann Jones-Harris for 59 years. Laura Ann Jones-Harris was born in Goochland County, Virginia in 1827. She and Peter had nine children.

54.) William Harris (Picture) William was the oldest son of Peter and Laura Ann Jones-Harris and the grandson of Joseph "FreeJoe" and Fanny Harris. He was also a circuit preacher and a co-founder of the all Negro town, Mound Bayou, Mississippi.

55.) A typical plate setting during the 1800's.

Information on the exhibit and the sale of pictures of all the 3-dimensional displays are available by writing or calling:

FreeJoe Enterprises
P. O. Box 280786
Memphis, Tennessee 38168
Telephone: (901) 373-4770
Fax: (901) 373-4770

Order Form

"FreeJoe"
A Story of Love, Faith and Perserverance

(hardback)

Please send me___copies of FreeJoe at $27.95 per copy $_____

Shipping and Handling $____4.00____

Total $_____

Rush the order to:

Name:_____

Address;_____

City:_____State_____

Zip Code:_____

Send Check or Money Order to:

**FreeJoe Publications
A Division of FreeJoe Enterprises
P.O. Box 280786
Memphis, Tennessee 38168
Telephone (901) 373-4770
Fax (901) 373-4770**

Note: Libraries, Bookstores and Universities that prefer not to order from the publisher, may order from our National Distributor:

**Baker and Taylor
44 Kirby Avenue
Somerville, N.J. 08876-0734
(908) 722-8000**